THE SMALL BUSINESS COMPUTER BOOK

A GUIDE IN PLAIN ENGLISH

Robert A. Moskowitz

UPSTART PUBLISHING COMPANY, INC.
The Small Business Publishing Company
Dover, New Hampshire

Published by Upstart Publishing Company, Inc.
A Division of Dearborn Publishing Group, Inc.
12 Portland Street
Dover, New Hampshire 03820
(800) 235-8866 or (603) 749-5071

Neither the author nor the publisher of this book is engaged in rendering, by the
sale of this book, legal, accounting or other professional services. The reader is
encouraged to employ the services of a competent professional in such matters.

Library of Congress Cataloging-in-Publication Data
Moskowitz, Robert.
     The small business computer book : a guide in plain English /
Robert A. Moskowitz
           p. cm.
     Includes bibliographical references and index.
     ISBN 0-936894-44-X : $19.95
     1. Small business--Data processing. 2. Small business--
Automation . 3. Microcomputers--Purchasing. I. Title.
HF5548.2.M6754   1993
     658'.05--dc20   93-14980
                                                            CIP

Cover design by Acanthus Graphic Design, Newington, NH.

Printed in the United States of America
10 9 8 7 6 5 4 3 2 1

For a complete catalog of Upstart's small business publications, call (800) 235-8866.

Dedication

To my wife, children and friends, who unflinchingly gave me all their support throughout the long process of researching, writing, testing and refining the information in this book.

Table of Contents

1

Why Business Loves Computers

This book is really not about computers. It's about business—and how to operate your business better, faster, more efficiently and effectively. Computers can bring you a great deal of improvement. But in the process of switching to computers, many organizations have learned that the largest gains come not only from raw computer power, but from thinking and planning how to conduct their businesses more efficiently. In other words, even before they computerize, they begin to benefit from the work-flow streamlining they must do in preparation for effectively converting to computers.

In this chapter, you'll learn in very general terms how computers can help a business operate. In the next chapter, you'll begin examining your own business to see where computerization can be valuable. With this solid basis of understanding, you'll then be able to work through the following chapters on software and hardware to determine exactly what computer products you want and need.

In this book, I won't be supplying you with specific brand names, product specifications, or even recommendations about your business computer requirements. Instead, I'll be helping you identify the correct questions to ask computer suppliers and consultants, and giving you the practical tools to identify the best answers for your particular business situation.

When first introduced in the late 1940s and early 1950s, computers were primarily a novelty and a scientific tool. The greatest scientists of the age predicted that four or five of the new computers would provide sufficient data processing power to meet all the needs of the entire United States.

Clearly, they were terribly wrong.

Today there are hundreds of millions of computers busily storing information, manipulating data, projecting future trends, generating words and pictures, and otherwise doing a mind-boggling assortment of tasks. As a result, nearly everyone on the planet is touched in some way by the power of computers to interact with the everyday drama of human life.

Nowhere is this impact more profound or ubiquitous than in the world of business.

THE USE OF COMPUTERS IN BUSINESS

There are several reasons computers have become so popular for business applications. The most often cited advantages are increased productivity and efficiency, particularly among white collar and professional workers. In thousands of organizations, accountants, lawyers, designers, managers, and people in many other positions use computers to handle more information, automate repetitive tasks, and otherwise accomplish more work in less time.

Although some studies have found little in the way of improved productivity or increased efficiency among those working with computers, I suspect a far more likely explanation for any apparent lack of improvement results from design flaws in the studies, rather than a failure of computers to help people accomplish more work. I'm so certain of this because I can personally testify to major productivity and efficiency increases that result directly from using a computer. For example, while writing this paragraph I was interrupted by a telephone call from someone who wanted a bit of information. During the brief conversation, the woman who called gave me the address of an organization in an industry I'm eager to explore. I immediately used my computer to modify an existing inquiry letter, adding the organization's name and address, and printing the letter and an envelope to match. Doing all that on the computer was so quick and easy I was able to come back to writing this paragraph without losing my original train of thought. What's more, by simply typing the address of that organization into the computer, I was able to print both the letter and the envelope, and also permanently store the information where I can quickly find it again and make use of it any time I want.

Without a computer, writing that letter would have required much more thought and effort, and taken much longer. It almost certainly would have interrupted my chain of thought on this book, wasting even more of my time. Conceivably, the need to finish these paragraphs would have stopped me from writing the letter, thereby preventing potentially wonderful opportunities from occurring.

The kind of productivity I'm describing is terribly difficult to measure or identify in standard time-and-motion studies. But it is very real and practical, and it often translates immediately and directly into extra dollars in sales and profits. I know hundreds of people who have begun to let computers generate organizational charts, retype letters and memos, search for particular facts or documents, calculate financial figures, remember customers' names and birth dates, and otherwise lighten the burden of day-to-day work so they can concentrate on the more important aspects of their business.

Aside from productivity increases, computers can easily store large amounts of data and process that data at very high speeds. The time and trouble of maintaining, for example, 1,000 or 15,000 names on a mailing list by using a computer is only a small fraction of what would be required to do the same work by hand. Thus, computers make it possible for organizations to grow larger and faster than they could without automation, and for people to tackle projects far larger than they would attempt without computer assistance.

For example, political fund raising has become a high art in recent years, primarily because computers have allowed fund-raisers to juggle, judge and respond to tiny demographic details among millions of potential contributors. The result can be a carefully targeted letter to contributors that names their neighbors and encourages each person to get others involved too. Such massive but individualized mailings are impossible without computers and are invaluable because they can persuade thousands more people to give millions more dollars than they would without the letter. No one can realistically quantify the increase in productivity or effectiveness such computer capabilities deliver.

Fortunately, the scale doesn't have to be large for computers to offer significant help. Whether it's dealing with one hundred or one hundred thousand items, computers are equally adept at balancing accounting transactions, tracking parcels in transit around the world, or continuously monitoring inventory levels of parts and materials and reordering anything that falls into short supply.

The average insurance agent, for example, can use a computer to provide potential clients with a sophisticated rate quote in a matter of minutes rather than days, making it easier and faster to sell insurance. The insurance agent can also use a computerized system to generate a list of impending expiration dates, and can even print individualized reminders or sales letters for each customer, just in time for his or her renewal.

Computers—despite their direct costs for hardware and software and the large additional investments we make in building databases and training people to use them—can greatly reduce the cost of doing business. At the simplest level, computerized records can replace paper documents, not only saving the cost of all that paper but the space and filing cabinets required to store it. For example, six "floppy" storage disks, which together occupy about the same space as a deck of playing cards, and which cost less than one dollar each, can contain the same information as 3,000 to 4,000 sheets of typing paper. Storage densities ten to one hundred times greater than this are also available with the right computer equipment. Higher speed "hard" disks costing a few hundred dollars, for example, can store the equivalent of 30,000 to 40,000 sheets of typing paper in a space no bigger than two decks of playing cards. And higher cost models about the same size can store two, three, four or five times as much material!

Computers deliver even greater savings when you start retrieving some of the information you have stored. Imagine you have that stack of 40,000 pages in your office, and you're trying to find a particular document. Even if you know right where to look, you'll spend precious time just getting to that file drawer to find the correct folder. And you must still locate the particular document you want. But a computer can scan the entire list of documents—potentially thousands of names—in a few seconds. If you can't recall the name of the document, you can have the computer search the contents of all the documents—word by word—in minutes and show you all the documents that meet your search criteria.

With today's image-management systems, you can not only pull up a file containing the text of the document you seek; you can view and reprint an exact replica of that document, complete with photos, graphics, pencil notations and smudge marks!

Computer technology provides cost savings by creating a world of simulations. At the high end, airline and military pilots can now complete much of their flight training in multimillion dollar computerized flight simulators that let them fly, crash and fly again without wrecking an airplane or burning a drop of jet fuel. Auto companies can "crash" dozens of cars in a computerized simulator to study auto safety and the behavior of components in various types of accidents without causing any actual damage. Aerospace vendors can "see" what it takes to break a jet engine turbine blade at high speed and high altitude entirely through computer simulations, and see it over and over again in slow motion if they wish. Although such simulators are extremely expensive, the savings make them very cost-effective.

As you might expect, smaller scale computers provide the same kinds of savings opportunities for the average business. For example, electronic spreadsheets provide a means of electronically "simulating" a financial transaction or a business deal well in advance of signing any papers. I know one real estate developer who constructed an entire skyscraper project inside a computer's electronic spreadsheet. From the purchase of the land through the signing of the final office lease, he projected the financial liabilities, expenses, cash flow, and profit potential at all stages of the project. He liked to say that before he turned a single spadeful of dirt, he knew exactly how much money he would make from the whole project. Clearly, such detailed simulations can help a business person make far better decisions than he or she could make without one.

The beauty of these financial simulations is that the computer model can become more complex than your own understanding of the situation. For example, in calculating the impact of restructuring your debt or refinancing your home, you can easily consider such details as:

- The direct costs of your planned refinancing or restructuring.
- The interest expense of the new debt compared with the existing debt.
- The impact of likely interest-rate scenarios on the costs of the new debt.
- The tax consequences of the decision.
- The results of restructuring a second time after just one, two, or three years, if you suddenly need to.

Your mind probably cannot consider all of these factors simultaneously. Yet after you build these considerations—one at a time—into your computer's spreadsheet, the computer retains them all and can show you their individual *and cumulative* impact all at once.

Aside from all this, computers are popular in business because they are a tool for developing entirely new capabilities. For example, bank and credit card loan officers often have great difficulty quantifying exactly how much credit to risk on a particular applicant. Some loan officers steadily accumulate a much better track record than others. Today's computerized systems can incorporate the experience and judgment of the best loan officers into an "artificial intelligence" system that other loan offices or officers can learn to consult and rely on, automatically making their judgments more accurate.

Today there are many computerized "presentation" programs that take long lists of numbers and turn them into vivid charts and business graphics. Long, difficult, highly detailed reports can be easily formatted and made more accessible with fancy typefaces, bold and italic print, justified margins, and automatically generated tables of contents and indexes. Some people keep their schedules on computerized calendar programs, and cannot only manage their time better, but can also have the computer automatically schedule meetings at a time when everyone invited is free to attend.

In the office, computer networks permit everyone to enter and retrieve data from wherever they are working. People in a task force or work group, for example, can share a single set of data files. This means everyone can contribute to a report or access a database without any of the expected problems, such as subtly differing versions, out of date copies, or files with conflicting data.

Computers are also quite good at supporting "long distance" activities, often called "telework" or "telecommuting." If your computer is equipped to communicate over telephone lines, you can work in a hotel room or bedroom far from the home office, yet send and receive data files and computerized messages—called "electronic mail"—as quickly as if you were just down the hall. This allows executives, sales people and others to stay in closer touch, better utilize more of the resources of the home office, and be more productive with computers than without them.

One of the most exciting ways computers help business is by fostering tighter integration with customers and suppliers. Ideally, a customer's order automatically flows through his computer system to yours, where it immediately triggers an order for the work to be done. Information also flows automatically from your computer system to your suppliers', where it alerts them to ship any required raw materials or parts you need to complete your customer's orders. So far, few companies are this tightly integrated, but any level of computerized information sharing cuts costs and helps expand your penetration into a particular market. Computer integration also gives companies an incentive to continue doing business with your firm.

Ways You Can Use a Computer

Like most machines, a computer is simply a tool. But unlike a hammer or an airplane, tools that have relatively limited uses, you can easily use a computer in many different ways: as a simple tool to compute mathematical formulas, as a resource to simplify and support business activities, as a management aide to improve decision-making, as a research laboratory to investigate new ideas or possibilities, and more. In fact, with the development of today's high-level programming languages, computers can be used for virtually anything you can imagine. And when they break, they make great boat anchors too.

So that you may begin to visualize, plan, evaluate and select your own computer system, here is a brief discussion of some of the more common uses for computers in business today.

Each usage discussed below is made possible by computer "software"—or programming commands—a complete package of which takes control of a computer and allows it to provide specific services and perform certain specific functions. In practice, you can use the same computer for many different software-controlled functions, although the more exotic ones may require special hardware devices too.

Be aware that software is written for a particular brand or class of computer. For example, software written for Apple Macintosh won't run on IBM and IBM-compatible personal computers, or on the NEXT computer. Most software is for computers using DOS or Windows or System 7 or UNIX. Because computers vary in their hardware and software potential and present capabilities, every software package will not necessarily work on every brand or class of computer on the market. Thus, your choice of software and hardware must be carefully coordinated. For now, though, just consider the possibilities.

Accounting

One of the most obvious, traditional and effective uses for computer power is handling the tedious, time-consuming, and prone-to-error work involved in ordinary accounting.

Hundreds of computer programs are available for dozens of different types and sizes of computer systems. Basically, they all do the same thing: keep track of money owed, money paid, and money received under a more or less complex chart of accounts. The simplest systems are little more than checkbook balancers, while the most sophisticated ones allow banks to operate automatic teller machines all over the nation and the world. Sophisticated accounting packages include sections for inventory management, project accounting, asset management, loan management, and many other highly specialized functions that are absolute necessities in certain business situations.

In between, there are a great many practical choices that provide you with all you might require in the way of work stations, transaction speed and capacity, power to crunch numbers and track accounts, and on-screen displays or hardcopy printouts.

There are both "general" software packages designed to do accounting for virtually any type of operation and transaction, and "vertical" software packages specifically designed for a single industry, such as government contractors, manufacturing, distribution or retailing. "Retail" software packages, for instance, are set up with an emphasis on recording and tracking each sale, and also on managing such important facets of the business as inventory, ordering, price markdowns, payroll and sales taxes.

Accounting software can also help you keep track of your business' performance for any period, and help you aggregate this performance not only among several periods but among several separate operations, such as among all the product lines of a company or among your personal and business expenses.

Planning and Decision Making

Accounting deals primarily with real money. There are other programs better equipped to handle *hypothetical* money—the kind you work with when you plan a new venture or consider the pros and cons of particular financial decisions.

For example, working with a computerized mortgage amortization system would allow you to quickly calculate and compare the costs of many different mortgages or business loans you might be considering. Some financial planning software packages make it easier for you to compare the alternatives as you develop a strategy of investment for your retirement, while investment tracking or portfolio management software might simplify the work of keeping detailed records on your various properties, stocks, and bonds, and of accounting for the income, expenses, depreciation, and appreciation associated with each one.

Financial planning can be as simple as calculating the present value of an anticipated income stream from, say, a government bond, or as complex as using current sales data from your business to project trendlines and calculate optimum inventory levels and operating cash requirements six months ahead. Today's software is so well developed you can use your computer for virtually any financial calculations, projections or tracking you might need.

Writing

After accounting and number crunching, "text editing" or "word processing" is one of the most well-established, traditional and commonplace applications for computer power. According to a recent survey, more than 85 percent of business PCs (personal computers) have software for word processing already installed or readily available.

The first "text editors" were simple tools for editing lines of words and numbers. They were designed and created by computer programmers to help them write more complex software. But today's text editors have come a long way. Not only can you use word processors to enter letters and numbers, copy and move them around inside your file, and erase the ones you don't want, you can also control such niceties as pagination, typefaces and type sizes, margins, bullets, line drawing, data tables, mathematical equations, business graphics, and much, much more.

Many word processors offer a dictionary, thesaurus, and/or grammar checking capability. Most either include or are compatible with a "macro" capability that makes it easy to reenter difficult names or any sequence of keystrokes. For example, easily programmed macros let you add your return address with a single keystroke or capture any unusual spelling and then retype it any number of times without a mistake.

Word processors can be used for everyday correspondence, memos and notes. They work fine for drafting and printing detailed reports, proposals, contracts, descriptive materials and "boilerplate" text you'll want to use over and over again.

Once you start using a word processor, it's simple to improve much of your business writing by reusing previous material that has worked well for you. You can start with a copy of a professionally pre-written letter, then simply add the appropriate details and make the appropriate changes or deletions to "make the letter your own." Or you can use the best of your own previous writing as the starting point. Since you don't begin with a blank page, you finish your writing much faster and easier than you would without the computer.

Publishing

Since the early 1980s, the most advanced word processors have grown in power and become sufficiently versatile to be thought of as "mini-publishers" or "desktop publishers." These software packages have many more features to handle graphics, page formatting, text sizing and other details for very precise control of the printed page.

By using style sheets or other advanced styling capabilities, these "publishing" programs take you far beyond simple letter writing. They let you create product-oriented newsletters, sales flyers, store signs, presentation charts and other attractively formatted materials for which the text you write is just the starting point.

Of course, these programs are not a substitute for talent or understanding page design—and they have so many features and nuances they can be difficult to master—yet they make it relatively quick and easy to give a professionally-designed look to much of your printed materials. In fact, once you have developed—or paid someone to develop for you — one or more standard "styles," you can apply them automatically to new text you write on your computer. The result is great-looking printed pages produced with a minimum of time and effort.

Desktop publishers are so cost-effective they already directly replace, or soon will, the time-honored traditions of mechanical typesetting and manual page layout that have produced virtually all the books, magazines, brochures, newspapers and other printed materials we read.

Managing Information

Because the computer is so quick at scanning large volumes of material and picking out the exact information you seek, it's a wonderful tool for handling reference information. More and more libraries are converting to computerized catalogs as replacements or augmentations for the traditional card catalogs. As computerized storage media become faster, more capacious, and less expensive, we'll see a steady increase in offerings along the lines of computerized encyclopedias, telephone books, dictionaries, legal references and specialized industrial lists such as patents, chemicals and books-in-print.

Publishing in electronic form rather than on paper has become so inexpensive that subscriptions to monthly magazines on disk have been marketed, and many companies regularly publish their phone directories, product listings or other frequently referenced information on CDs (compact disks) or other high-speed, read-only media. Even without this capability, there are many opportunities to store and manage information in your computer.

Databases

One of the most common uses for computers is to manage large quantities of data. As I've noted, you can enter and store virtually any information you wish for use with a word processor. Once it's in your computer, you can ask the word processor to search for the text you want, and you then view, edit or print the material from that portion of your word processing data file. But as the volume of data increases, this becomes a very cumbersome approach. It's much faster and more efficient to provide a more organized scheme for storing the data. This is where computerized databases, and database manager software packages, come in.

A database is a computer-age term for any collection of information. A database can include all your customers and their history of purchases, a mailing address or telephone listing, or anything else. Technically, your word processing file is a database. But in practice, a computerized database is usually marked by a high degree of organization that supports very rapid retrieval of its information. Database management software acts on such database files, and, with a few simple keystrokes, provides an easy means of searching for any particular piece of information or any combination of pieces of information, as well as sorting and manipulating part or all of the database.

For example, a computerized mailing list can easily be sorted into ZIP code order and printed on labels, saving considerably on postage. A computerized telephone directory can be searched at electronic speeds to find a particular person's number, can even dial it for you automatically—if your computer has a modem—and, if the number is busy, continue to redial until you get through.

Databases also increase productivity by centralizing information storage and letting people use each piece of data many times. For instance, once you enter a customer's name into your database, you can retrieve that same information and use it on every invoice, every shipping label, every collection letter, every direct mail solicitation, every catalog and every Christmas card. If the name and address are correctly entered, they'll be correct every time they're printed. If you make a change once, from then on you'll automatically use the new version every time.

Statistics
Another general use for database managers is for statistical analysis. Loaded with a database of customers and the products they buy, for example, your computer can calculate the percentage of purchasing that takes place each month or each season, the contribution of each customer's purchases to total sales of each product, or each customer's seasonal pattern of purchasing.

Databases of sales, inventory or other actual business performance can be operated upon to provide trends and a detailed picture of operations, cash flow and profitability. For example, it's easy to have the computer report how well each product sells in each state, or what products are generating the greatest portion of overall profits. By combining a product sales database with a customer-demographics database, you can investigate exactly who buys which of your products—and thus formulate better plans for selling more to each cluster of your customers.

With years of performance data computerized, it's also possible to make reliable projections for expected performance during future months, quarters and years. You can have the computer perform complex statistical studies in minutes that would take hours to do by hand. Statistical analysis can help you determine the best ways to keep inventories low but adequate, gear up for peak sales or production periods, develop incentives and procedures to increase relatively weak lines of business operations, and find new opportunities based on current successes.

Project Management
Computers are also valuable aids in project management, where they can be of major assistance in scheduling and planning the allocation of human and other resources. Word processing, database management, electronic spreadsheet and highly specific project management software all can be utilized to help you understand and control all the efforts necessary to bring a project to a successful conclusion.

All the daily activities, subtasks, and tasks involved in the project can be listed in the computer, and then sorted, selected and printed to create a project "flow chart." When the inevitable delays, changes and mistakes alter the original plan, the computer makes it far easier than it would be by hand to simply modify the computer file and reprint a new flow chart. And as various activities, subtasks, and tasks are completed, they can be hidden or marked within the computer software so subsequent displays or print-outs help you easily focus your attention on what remains to be done.

Project management software and some applications using database management software permit tasks to be linked to specific people, specific dates and specific resources such as supplies or materials, locations and so forth. The software then permits the computer user to reshuffle the file and view all the work associated with certain people, dates, resources or certain locations. Other software features allocate the right people, resources, time and money to specific aspects of the project automatically, without requiring manual entries.

The net effect of automated project management is that project managers and decision makers can spend far less time on the mechanical business of noting allocations, changes and other details. Instead, they can use the computer's power and speed to gain a faster, deeper understanding of the project in any and all of its phases. They can also use it to make presentations to those in charge of funding—or those whose cooperation they need—to facilitate completion of the project on time and on (or under) budget.

Presentations and Graphics

Computers are good not only at manipulating information but at printing it on paper, or preparing it for placement on slides or overhead transparencies, or for rapid display on the computer's own monitor or on a special transparent monitor that lets you project the computer's display image onto a wall or a movie screen. As a result, a computer is an uncommonly good tool for presenting information quickly, vividly and persuasively.

"Presentation" software enables a computer to quickly generate large-type slides or printed pages complete with arrows, bullets, boxes, and other graphic elements to make the information very accessible. Many packages allow you to use "style sheets," so every page in the presentation automatically takes on the uniform look of a cohesive whole. If you choose to print the presentation, some packages will also print "notes" pages on which you can jot reminders to yourself as you lead others through the presentation. If you're going to speak to a large group, it may also be possible to print "handouts" that contain four, six, or even eight of your presentation pages on each sheet.

Many presentation packages offer a "slide show" option that allows you to prepare a series of on-screen displays and organizes them into a complete, carefully-timed "show." You can load this show onto virtually any computer and trigger the entire sequence of displays with a single keystroke, or simply press a button repeatedly to move from one slide to another at your own pace. By replacing the normal computer display with a computerized transparency, you can project the slide show on a large screen for easy viewing by your audience.

More sophisticated software permits a degree of animation, so one screen can dissolve into another, words and numbers can fade in or out of view, or an arrow can move across the screen and pierce the object to which it is pointing. Adding such features to a presentation can give it a lot more impact than standard, frozen images would give.

Of course, once a computerized presentation is prepared, it's relatively easy to update with the latest figures, or to change a few words here and there to make it suitable for a different client or prospect. It's also possible to use the old presentation as a "template" for a new one, so it's easier to have all your presentations maintain a consistent look or corporate identity.

Forms

Though we can't fully automate every business operation, one area that's not only very easy to automate but extremely cost-effective and profit-enhancing as well, is the design, printing, distribution and storage of forms. All the popular drawing programs, including the more specialized "forms design" software, let you create and modify the lines and text for any form within the computer until you get it right. Once you're satisfied, you can print it and make duplicates conventionally, or print enough originals from the computer for a day or a week. This avoids large printing bills, inventory storage and management requirements, and wasted money when you inevitably update the form and relegate to wastepaper thousands of copies you've bought and paid for.

Because forms must be filled in and reviewed, computers help you become even more productive when you start automating this part of the process. The computer can check to make sure everyone is filling things in correctly, like putting dates, part numbers and pricing in the right places on the form. The computer can also complete the blanks. Once someone enters a customer name, for example, the computer can "fill-in" the correct address and phone number automatically. It can do the same with part numbers, descriptions, pricing or anything else it can find on a prepared list.

The computer can also perform math or logical computations. On a sales form, for example, if you specify five units at $15.95, the computer can immediately "fill in" the extension: $79.75. When you've entered every item, the computer can quickly figure the subtotal, itemize the sales tax and shipping charges, then compute and display the total amount due.

The most important part of working with forms is not printing or filling them in, but reading, analyzing and acting upon the information the forms contain. In all these areas, inexpensive software lets your computer provide a great deal of extra help. In fact, once you have computerized the information on your forms, it's relatively easy to feed it into a database or spreadsheet program for high-speed manipulations and analysis.

Training
There are several ways in which computers can significantly cut the costs or improve the quality of individual training programs. First, many software programs provide their own automated training. This can be in the form of menus or dedicated "tutorial" programs.

Second, computers can be used to train a person in any particular area of knowledge or job performance. With the rapidly developing technology for interactive training, the computer shows a trainee carefully developed still images or moving pictures and underscores the training message with on-screen graphics, stop-motion and special effects. To succeed, trainees are expected to respond with the right answers or computer keystrokes. Training developers can program the computer to ask questions, record and score responses, and use each trainee's demonstrated mastery of certain material as the basis for selecting his or her next topic.

Where Computers Fit and Where They Don't

Obviously, computers are very powerful tools for improving productivity and effectiveness. But there are some areas in which they can be more useful than others. Here are some guidelines for finding places in your own work where computers can be helpful:

For Repetitive Tasks

Computers excel at doing a particular thing over and over again. If you must repeat the same processes and actions, and reuse words or numbers—paying monthly bills, writing letters with the same information, calculating the same math equations, or anything similar—you can probably get done faster with the use of a computer.

For Rapid Access to Information

Computers are extremely fast at combing one or more data files in search of a particular sequence of letters and numbers. If you find yourself searching for specific details in a large database (remember, that's any collection of information), you can probably find it faster by computerizing the information and searching electronically.

For Graphics

Many small businesses—and even a few large ones—never develop a formal organization chart and are satisfied with reports prepared on a typewriter. They do quite well without slide shows or animated presentations of any kind. To be sure, there is no imperative—at least not yet—to incorporate the use of graphics in basic business operations. But as an audience, we've grown used to seeing graphics in professionally made movies, television shows and printed pieces. This increasing sophistication of the average reader/viewer, coupled with the growing complexity of business situations and decisions—and the already frequent use of graphics by competitors and by leading firms—are inducing more and more business people to rely on graphics to:

- make issues clearer,
- make information and ideas more vivid and easier to understand,
- create a stronger, more professional impression of their company,
- clarify difficult or complex relationships, and
- just attract the eye of the beholder.

For Advanced Calculations
Computers are adept at mathematical computations. That's why electronic spreadsheets, accounting programs, and other math-oriented software packages are natural choices for computer uses. If you frequently compute the answers to mathematical formulas (as simple as 2 + 2 or as complex as sophisticated statistical and financial calculations can become), you can certainly make better use of your time by putting the calculations into your computer.

To Support Workers
Modern technology allows computers not only to repeat simple tasks, find information, and do math, but to provide a measure of support for judgments and decisions that workers are required to make. With "artificial intelligence" software, today's computers are able to increase the level of performance of the average person by supplying some of the experience, expertise and advanced judgment that recognized experts bring to particular jobs: chemical analysis, bank and credit lending, medical diagnosis, business management and other specialties. If you make or need others to make critical decisions on complex issues, it may be possible to provide automated support that improves productivity and effectiveness in these efforts.

To Capture Data for EIS
One of the areas where up-to-the-minute data can be crucial is business management and decision making. There's a growing emphasis on EIS (Executive Information Systems), which gather and present detailed pictures of business operations as simply and succinctly as possible to those in key positions of control. But these systems do little good unless the information is both current and complete. By adding computers everywhere from retail point-of-sales to manufacturing shop floors, from loading docks and shipping bays to purchasing offices and inventory storerooms, management can monitor and analyze operations and trends as situations develop, bringing significant benefits well beyond any direct improvements in these operational areas.

For example, restaurant chains can use computerized cash registers to record data on items sold every day at each location, then transmit that information to headquarters, where analysts can plot trends, analyze sales and replenish each restaurant's inventories. Supermarkets are also becoming skilled at tracking sales, analyzing demographic databases, and making better decisions on which products to carry, push, and drop from their shelves. By computerizing such day-to-day operational information, business organizations can load their EIS with hard data with which top management can make far better decisions.

STRATEGIC ADVANTAGES OF COMPUTERS IN BUSINESS

We've already discussed the most well-known and easily understood advantages of using computers: increased productivity and effectiveness, increased capabilities for individuals and the organization as a whole, cost effective data processing, and overall tighter management of the business. But there is another improvement only now beginning to be well understood: the use of information as a strategic advantage.

Large organizations like Corning Glass, Xerox, and Chevron Chemical are seeking to use their data processing capabilities to make them more attractive to their customers and gain better service and lower prices from their suppliers. Of course, these same possibilities exist on a much smaller scale for smaller organizations. Adding computer power to the way you do business can allow you to outperform your competition and offer value-added services your customers cannot obtain anywhere else.

For example, tracking your customers' purchases can allow you to print reports that show their purchasing history or predict when they will run short of supplies and need to reorder. Internally, such information can help you make sure *you* don't run short of what your customers are likely to order. You can also share your information with customers, and thus help them monitor and control their purchasing—at least with your company. One specialty bakery has been successful in offering a year-end summary of each customer's purchases, sorted by delivery address as well as by month. The summary makes it very easy for customers to send year-end gifts to their clients and friends. Because the data is already available in the bakery's computerized system, the cost of providing the summary is relatively low. Yet the perceived value is relatively high.

It's also possible to link your accounting systems with those of your customers and/or suppliers. Thus, when you generate an invoice, it's automatically transmitted and entered as a payable item on your customer's accounting system. Similarly, when your suppliers bill you, the items are automatically entered for payment. As this integration grows in sophistication, you can begin to monitor your customer's inventory levels and replace those in short supply, and your suppliers can do the same for you.

In health care, data processing systems are increasingly linked together so a bill generated by a doctor or a hospital is immediately passed through a bill-monitoring company and on to the federal government or private insurance company that will ultimately pay it by making an electronic transfer into the service provider's bank account. Paper is not eliminated, but it is greatly reduced, as is the time required to process the whole transaction.

Aside from the performance and cost advantage of integrated computer systems, don't lose sight of the strategic advantage: once a company is integrated with your computer systems, it tends to become far less likely to want to go elsewhere.

Another strategic advantage computers can bring is the improvement in response times they make possible. For example, in many firms there's a two, three or even four week delay between the time an order or request is received and the time it is fulfilled. By computerizing the "order processing" sequence, many companies not only make improvements to paper-based systems, but find ways to speed up and streamline the process that actually cuts weeks off their response times. This inevitably makes them more competitive than rivals that are not computerized.

All this only scratches the surface of possibilities as computer software, hardware, and experience continues to expand with amazing rapidity.

LIABILITIES OF USING COMPUTERS

Despite their tremendous advantages, computers have liabilities too. There is a saying among computer users you would do well to remember: "To err is human; to really foul up requires a computer." Because computers are so fast, so powerful, and so capable of dealing with large quantities of information, a small error by a computer can quickly escalate into a major mishap.

In addition, computers are so useful that organizations generally grow very dependent upon them. For example, if you computerize your order processing department, you will probably experience significant improvements in productivity. But then if the computer system fails— even in the simplest way—your entire order processing department may lose a day's work or more. The old method of doing things by hand will no longer make sense, and operations can grind to a halt.

Also, data stored on a computer is subject to being lost or rendered unusable in an instant (that's why you always back-up any programs and data you cannot afford to lose). There are other potential liabilities as well.

Fear of Computers

Although less prevalent than when computers first began appearing in business organizations, computer-phobia can still create problems in an otherwise happy, peaceful scene. Computers need not be complicated, and with menus and graphical user interfaces, they can be made downright simple to operate. But people may nevertheless fear them.

With good reason, employees may feel afraid that a computer will eliminate their position in the organization, or that they will not be able to learn how to use the computer and will therefore be replaced by someone who can. People may also feel afraid for more complex, psychological reasons that effectively hamper their productivity when a computer is involved.

High Start-Up Cost

The initial expense, of course, depends on your requirements for a computer system, and on your perspective. Perfectly adequate personal computers are available for less than $500. Compared with the million-dollar price tags of computers in the 1960s and 1970s, this is dirt-cheap. But if you're starting a business with total capital of $1,000, a computer may be far too expensive.

Also, computer systems can cost quite a bit more than $500 when you begin to pay for extra speed, more memory, larger storage capacity, and better printer or display options. Computers capable of architectural or engineering design work, for example, can cost $10,000 or more. In fact, there's virtually no upper limit on how much you can spend for a computer. Generally, the challenge is to buy only as much capability as you will regularly use.

Whatever the price tag, computers require an immediate outlay of time and money, and pay back this investment over a long period. Although you cannot dodge the start-up costs of automating some of your business, computers can be so supportive of increased efficiency, productivity and strategic advantage, that they will frequently pay for themselves in the first few months of operation.

Start-Up Problems and Delays

Once a computer is set up to do the tasks you require, it will normally remain a very reliable and cost-effective system. But getting the system to work right in the first place can be unreasonably expensive and time-consuming.

The simplest thing to do, of course, is turn on a standard computer, load a standard word processor or spreadsheet program, and start using it. That takes very little time, and you can be productive immediately.

But some applications take more preparation, for example, if you want to develop a spreadsheet to model a particularly complex financial transaction, you could spend many weeks getting it right. If you're using a database application to handle accounts or manage projects, you could spend months entering and checking all the information, and more months developing the reports and various screens for the application you want, before receiving any benefits from your effort or expense.

The most difficult situation is when you want the computer to do something very unusual, such as perform a task for which there is no "off-the-shelf" software. This requires custom programming, and thus the expense of proficient programmers. Custom programming always takes longer and costs more than you anticipate, and generally entails more problems and "bugs" to be removed than anyone expects. Rarely does the software work as well as it was intended to, and making changes often involves further delays and can create new problems in parts of the program that once worked perfectly. I've known plenty of small-business people who went out of business while they were trying to get custom software up and running. Clearly, it's very dangerous to depend on any projections of completion times or programming costs for custom computer applications.

Rapid Obsolescence

The most ironic liability of computer systems is their almost immediate obsolescence. Technology has been improving so fast that the computer you acquire today is likely to be superseded by a smaller, faster, more powerful or more capable one within a few months or a year. For many people considering their first computer, this is a paralyzing situation. But it shouldn't be.

Automobiles provide a good analogy. Even though you know next year will bring newer models with better features, you nevertheless understand the value of acquiring a car to meet your needs right now. Unfortunately, a used computer, like a used car, is worth only a fraction of what it originally cost. And software is worth even less, frequently as little as five or ten cents on the dollar.

But your biggest investment need not depreciate. This is the time you take training yourself—and others—to use the computer, and the time and effort spent creating and entering the data on which your computer operates. The hardware and software are very cheap compared to this central investment, and their rapid obsolescence, while distressing, should not diminish the benefits you continue to obtain from your data and your computerization.

DEALING WITH PROMINENT FACTORS IN THE ACQUISITION DECISION

Choosing a computer system wisely involves balancing many different factors, none of which should entirely dictate the final selection.

Falling prices are a fact of life in the world of computers. Today's $5,000 high-speed system is next month's $2,500 average computer. Acquisition decisions should not rest solely on the anticipated resale value of the computer when you replace it, but on the performance that a computer will deliver—and the advantages it will provide—during its entire useful life of two to five years.

Improved capability is the flip side of falling prices. Rather than raise prices for each new capability, computer vendors try to hold the line on prices and compete by adding new capabilities. Thus a $2,000 system from 1980 would cost only about $300 today. You can still spend $2,000 for a computer, but it has far more power than the 1980 model. Again, it's wise to buy all the capabilities you can use, and to buy a computer with at least a modest potential for expansion and increased capability as years go by.

An important but often overlooked consideration in deciding on a computer system is the longevity of the company from which you acquire it. If the company goes out of business, how will you obtain spare parts or upgrades to hardware and software that become obsolete? If you need help with compatibility problems, a defunct company will be of little use. This does not mean that you should deal only with the largest, strongest vendors. But it does suggest that you consider vendor viability as one factor when you select and acquire components for your computer system.

In large organizations, acquiring massive computer systems can be a major undertaking. But even if you're only buying a computer for word processing in a corner of your bedroom, you should consider factors like the quantity of data you will be processing, the quality of output you will need, the sources for input, the need for communications, preferences for on-screen displays, and so forth. Remember, the basis for your selection must be determined by your own computer performance requirements.

The general procedure for selecting computer systems is to determine your performance or operational requirements, select the software you need to meet those requirements, and then select the hardware needed to support the desired software. Going the other way—that is, choosing hardware and then finding software to meet your needs—usually works out to be a much less efficient, more frustrating, and potentially less satisfactory approach.

GROWING WITH COMPUTERS IN BUSINESS

Computers tend to be so useful in business that once you begin to use one, you'll probably want to add more and more power and capability. At the same time, your computer requirements may also be growing because you are expanding your business. Consequently, most organizations that acquire a single computer add more of them quickly. That's why it's important you consider issues of compatibility from the very beginning. Since your largest investment is in user training and the data entered into your computer(s), you won't want to start all over again whenever older computers aren't compatible with newer systems.

This urge to protect your existing investment in training and data is so strong that after six months or a year you probably won't want to change for anything. That's why it's important from the very beginning to consider issues of vendor viability and the possible "migration path" to newer, more capable systems. Older systems in which your investment is generally well protected because your existing training and data can be used with newer versions of the same products are called "upwardly compatible." "Downwardly compatible" systems are newer ones that allow you to utilize your existing data and training from older systems. Certain vendors and certain technologies tend to provide a great deal of upward compatibility, and these are much safer choices than those that may leave your investment at a dead end.

Since computer systems are always improving, the pressure to acquire newer, more capable systems is fairly steady and unremitting. But since changing computer systems every six months is often impractical, here are some guidelines for when to move up:

1) Move up to newer computer hardware or software when the move would be cost effective. That is, compare the advantages and benefits that will accrue from the new components or systems against the costs of making the move. Remember to include costs of retraining, moving data to the new system, productivity problems while people are learning the new system, bugs and other potential problems.

2) Move up to newer computer hardware or software when the move would eliminate problems or constraints that are more expensive than the cost of the move. For example, if productivity is limited by the current computer system's capacity, compare the cost of moving up to a better system against the opportunity cost—or foregone advantages—of continuing with the existing system.

3) Move up to newer computer hardware or software when the move would create or facilitate opportunities that outweigh the costs and potential pitfalls of the change. For example, a new computer system might create opportunities to compete in new areas, cut costs or improve collections. In deciding whether to make the changeover, compare the anticipated benefits against the known costs of the conversion.

Integrating Old Systems With New Systems

Aside from upward and downward compatibility, another important consideration is the ability to integrate the computer system you are selecting now with other systems you may select in the future. Integration is a complex technical matter too detailed to cover adequately in this book. As a practical matter, however, integrating two or more computer systems often depends on finding (or building) specific hardware or software products to provide that integration cost-effectively. Because successful integration is such a highly detailed and complex matter, it's far wiser to expect that two systems cannot be integrated—and perhaps to be pleasantly surprised when they can—than to expect easy integration, only to be sadly disappointed.

Overview of a Complete Computer System

A computer system consists of many different components, all of which must work together perfectly for the system to function. The hardware parts of a basic computer system include the following:

- Central Processor
- Memory
- Display
- Keyboard and Mouse
- Storage System
- Printer

For your convenience, these terms are defined in the glossary.

Each of these components is used at certain times to support or control computer functions. Some—like the central processor and memory—are involved in virtually all computer functions. Others—like the keyboard, the display, or the storage system—need not be.

In a typical computer operation, data flows from the keyboard or the mouse, or the storage system, into the computer's memory. From there it is acted upon by the central processor according to software instructions. The resulting information may be displayed on the computer screen, or printed or stored for later use.

As I mentioned before, by loading the computer with the appropriate software, you can make it function as a word processor, financial planner, project manager or any of a hundred other tools. But just having the computer perform word processing or accounting is not a guarantee of productivity improvements or cost efficiency. The computer must be integrated with the people and the organization to effectively support the appropriate projects and tasks. Otherwise, you're likely to waste a great deal of time, effort and expense.

One of the most ticklish aspects of integrating the computer and the organization is managing what technicians like to call the "operator/machine interface," or the "human interface." In a nutshell, this refers to the interaction of people and computers. What makes this interface so difficult to get right is that people tend to be far more flexible than computers, so people adjust their own work habits to compensate for a great many computer shortcomings, failures, flaws and outright errors. The result is generally a significant compromise in the productivity improvement the computer was originally expected to deliver. The better approach is to have the computer side of the "human interface" adjusted as much as possible to meet the needs and preferences of the people who are operating the computers. As you go through this book, you'll get a lot of ideas on exactly how to accomplish these adjustments.

COMPUTER FUNCTIONS

Here's a brief explanation of the functions most computers perform. By putting these functions together in various combinations and patterns, a computer can accomplish vast quantities of difficult and complex work.

Data Entry
Without data entry, the computer is like a blank slate waiting for someone to write on it. The computer accepts information entered through the keyboard, mouse, or electronic transfer.

Computing or Data Processing
The ability to add, subtract, multiply and divide at lightning speed is what makes the computer so powerful a tool. In fact, these operations—along with copying data from one place to another—are nearly all a computer ever does. But because numbers can stand for letters, dots in a picture, or electrical signals on control wires, and because they can even control how other numbers are manipulated, the computer can be made to process words, handle images, and control devices.

Displaying

People gather most of their information with their eyes, so computers are built to display information visually. They use the screen not only to display data, but to provide command choices and to indicate what the computer can do, as well as what it is going to do next. Good software provides so much information on the display screen that you can often learn to run a computer just by looking at the screen and trying each of the various command options it gives you.

Copying Data

A basic function of computers is to copy data. (When computers add, subtract, multiply and divide, they actually copy information from one part of their memory to another.) For this reason, computers are very fast at copying information in word processing files, database files, electronic spreadsheets, and other software applications. When a computer saves a file, it actually copies the data from its active memory to a long-term storage device. When it retrieves a file, it copies the data from long-term storage into its active memory. This process of copying is significant because it means the original data remains intact at least until the computer copies new information on top of the old. Computers can easily copy the contents of one file to a new, separate file, essentially creating a duplicate and allowing you to make tentative changes to either one of the files without fear of changing the other.

Files, File Saving and File Retrieval

Computers organize data into files. A file can contain a single character, a letter or memo, a picture, or a report hundreds of pages long. A file is not the same as a document, because you can have many documents in a single file, or many files containing parts of a single document. Computer files can also contain mailing lists or lists of other information. Application software like database managers or electronic spreadsheets generally store information in files using very elaborate codes that cannot be read directly by other applications.

Once information is entered into the computer, it can be retained for months or years by "saving" it as a file inside some form of long-term data storage device. The most common device is the disk. "Floppy" disks hold the equivalent of a few hundred pages of data. "Hard" disks operate faster than floppies and can hold the equivalent of thousands, hundreds of thousands, or even millions of pages of data.

For a computer to manipulate information, it must be in the machine's memory. To get it there, you must enter it or retrieve it from a saved file. Generally, the computer retrieves the entire file at once, although some software may use just a small portion of the file. When a computer "opens" or retrieves a saved file, it only copies the information from the storage device into its memory. The original file remains intact within the storage device.

Information in the computer's active memory can be manipulated freely without changing the stored file from which the information was copied. After you make changes, saving the altered file using the original file name will overwrite and destroy the original stored information. However, you can easily save the changed information using a new file name, thus creating a second file in storage that leaves the original version untouched.

Deleting Data

The computer can erase data from its memory or its long-term storage. But until it does both, the data can usually be retrieved. Even after a file has been deleted from long-term storage, it may be recoverable by special utility software, providing the computer has not written other information in the physical locations where the deleted file was stored.

Printing

We are so dependent on printed material that computers have been built with excellent paper-marking devices. Most of what computers print are "reports" that contain, explain or visually express the results of the data manipulation and analysis we perform with various software packages. But computers can also produce visual images, banners, calendars and more.

Communicating

Sending electronic signals along a wire is a basic function of computers equipped with the right hardware to do so. By connecting two or more similarly equipped computers, we can have them transfer data files, share printers, drives, and other devices, and even have one computer check on how well the other computer is performing.

2

Computerizing Your Business

As I said in Chapter 1, this book is not about computers. It's about business and using computers to do business more profitably and efficiently. It happens to contain a great deal of information about computers, but that's unavoidable. As your guide, I've taken great care to avoid talking about specific brands, model or version numbers, technologies or prices because in the computer industry these are quite likely to change from one season to the next. Knowing your business will be far more important in successfully introducing computers than studying to become a computer "techie." In fact, you don't need to know anything about computers to use them effectively in your business.

The basic process of how to go about computerizing a business involves taking the time to:

- identify the parts of your business you can most effectively computerize,
- improve and streamline those areas of your business for greater efficiency even before you start to computerize them,
- evaluate and select the most effective and appropriate computer system components, and
- manage the transition from the old system.

If you follow the proper steps in the correct order, computerizing your business will help you make it better managed, highly efficient, and more flexible and responsive to changing business demands. Your new computer system(s) will contribute in large measure to these improvements. But apart from any automation, your thinking and streamlining of business operations will be one of the most significant sources of improvement.

Before you begin to install a new computer system, you must examine your current day-to-day procedures. Pretend you're an outsider. Walk through the premises. Go over the operations. Talk to employees about what works and what doesn't. In the process you'll probably identify several—perhaps a great many—opportunities to eliminate redundancy, shorten the decision-making loops, streamline essential operations, reduce unnecessary overhead, and generally simplify procedures that have grown too complex. Inefficiencies of these types naturally spring up as you build and maintain a business, and, once in place, they tend to become solidified—"We've always done it that way"—until you consciously root them out.

One of the best times to address these problems is before you buy and install new computer systems. To computerize inefficient or outmoded procedures intact would be foolhardy and would add needless expense to the computerization project. Getting rid of inefficiencies first not only simplifies and lowers the cost of computerizing, it provides a running start on the road to profit improvement. This is why many organizations discover in their post-automation evaluations that the largest cost savings and productivity gains were realized not simply by installing a massive amount of computer power, but by carefully rethinking and planning daily business operations prior to computerizing them.

In this chapter, you'll begin examining your own business to see where computerization can be most valuable, and how to manage the transition from your present system to a more automated one. I won't be supplying you with the correct answers. Instead, I'll be helping you ask the right questions, and find your own answers that make the most sense for your particular business situation.

HOW TO IDENTIFY WHICH PARTS OF YOUR BUSINESS NEED COMPUTERS

Analyzing where and when to computerize business operations and processes is a lot simpler if you understand all the various parts of the business and how they fit together. Regardless of what your business actually does, most of the business operations and processes you will computerize are information-oriented: sales orders, names and addresses, part numbers, memos, correspondence, and so forth.

Computers can process information about anything, of course. They can guide a rocket ship to the moon, simulate the eruption of a volcano, track weather around the globe, or enhance pictures sent from the planet Uranus in the form of millions of bits of information. But these computers are considerably larger, more complex, and more expensive than the ones your business probably needs.

Not everything you computerize will be pure information, of course. You will probably consider computerizing the printing of bills, checks, correspondence and other paperwork. You may also computerize some graphic design and publishing work, or perhaps control ventilation and fire alarms in your building. As you continue to add automation to your business, you may set up computers to control elaborate manufacturing equipment. But for purposes of this analysis, any of these tasks will be considered a form of information processing.

A computer system generally looks like a few, simple, solid units. But in reality it is composed of millions of tiny hardware and software components. You can take this as an analogy to how a computer system must be applied to a business. It looks like you can just computerize the entire business at once. But in reality you must decide separately whether and when to computerize each small and separate business operation.

The easiest way to decide where and when to computerize is to work from a diagram that shows information and material flowing into, through, and out of the business. While taking time to conduct this type of analysis and draw a flow chart may seem tedious and unproductive, in practice you'll find it's a valuable exercise. It gives you a vivid picture of your organization that quickly reveals weak spots, bottlenecks, redundancies, and other problems.

Make a Flow Chart of Your Business
As you probably know, a flow chart is simply a diagram showing how information or material moves between the various operations or processes in your business. To make the chart most useful for your computerization study, it should indicate as many of the areas as possible where information or material first enters your company, and should follow it far enough to show where the processed information or material flows out again.

In the most general sense, business operations and processes include the flow of:

* money;
* goods, supplies, and raw materials;
* advertising, product descriptions, and other information;

- customer requests and purchases; and
- documentation mandated by business laws and regulations.

You may be able to think of other types of information that form, influence, or control important parts of your business. To help find them, go over in your mind all the people, things, and forces that impact your business. The most important of these should be expressed on your flow chart of business operations and processes. Your chart should also indicate how much time each process usually requires, and where delays occur as information or material goes from one process to the next. This timing data will help you identify areas where you'd like to speed up the flow of information or material in actual day-to-day operations.

For example, suppose a customer places a sales order on Monday, but little or nothing is done toward processing and filling that order until Tuesday. You've discovered a place where computers may improve efficiency. Or imagine that every afternoon 50 orders come to accounting that must be calculated and posted by hand before going out to the warehouse or shop floor for action. You've discovered a place where automation can eliminate a bottleneck.

Some studies of business computerization demonstrate that the actual flow of information or material through an organization is quite different from the "ideal" flow designed or imagined by owners, managers or consultants. If you find such discrepancies, chart both the hoped for and the actual processes. Later, you can choose which ones to computerize, based on your judgment of which ones seem likely to work best. You may spend fifteen minutes a day for weeks before you identify all the most important processes and pathways within your business. But, however long it takes, this analysis will pay tremendous dividends for years to come —regardless of whether or not you computerize.

To put some of these analytical concepts into a real-world context, let's look at an example of a typical retail store. Every day information and material flow into the business from a variety of sources. See figure 1 on page 34 for a sample of a flow chart for a retail store.

1) Requirements for bank deposits and monthly payments due flow "in" from the landlord or mortgage holder, utility companies and others to whom the store has contractual obligations.

2) The store's products and product information flow "in" from manufacturers and distributors. This helps establish what the store offers its customers.

3) Sales calls, product offerings, catalogs, and so forth flow "in" from the store's vendors. These create an environment of opportunity from which the store selects the offerings it will make to its customers.

4) Advertising and other communications flow "in" from competitors. I'm talking about your awareness of the competitive environment in which your store must survive.

5) Customers and potential customers ask questions and make requests for products and services, make complaints or ask for special options, make purchases, and tender payment for their purchases. These demands flow "in" and force you to respond appropriately, accurately, and in a timely manner.

6) Taxes, reporting requirements, and licensing or operating standards flow "in" from government and regulators. These dictate both behavior and financial expenditures.

But this is only the first part of the total "flow" that defines and describes your business. After all this information and material is received, it must be sorted and processed. The processing is generally what most people consider the active part of the business, but it's really only the most obvious and tangible portion of the total flow. The processing may go something like this:

1) Sales orders and revenues are entered into the accounting system along with payments due for rent, mortgage and utilities. These figures may also be factored into income projections and overhead or operating expenses for such purposes as planning, budgeting and pricing items sold in the store.

2) Vendor sales calls, product offerings, catalogs and other information are reviewed by the store manager for possible purchasing decisions. He or she may act immediately upon this information or may store it for future reference.

Figure 1

SAMPLE FLOW CHART OF A RETAIL STORE

Information and things entering the store

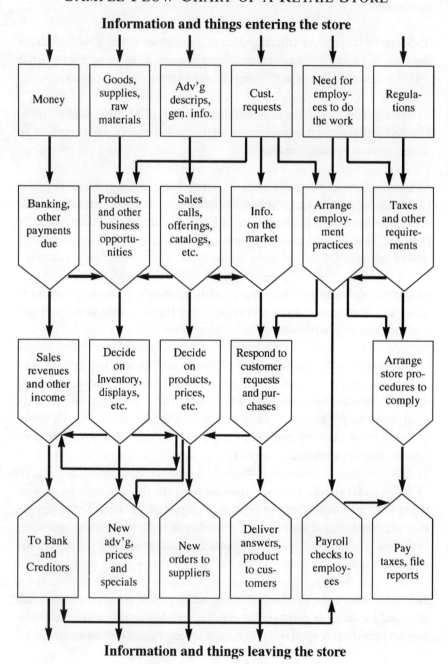

Information and things leaving the store

3) Competitors' advertising and other external communications form one basis for the retail store's own decisions on pricing, discounts, advertising and the like.

4) Products and product information are displayed in the store, placed in inventory, and/or entered into the store's accounting system as they enter through the receiving department and leave under customers' arms.

5) Questions and requests from customers and potential customers generate responses from sales people in the store, and may also filter up to management, where they may result in decisions to change the items in stock, adjust prices, offer special discounts or promotional programs, and so forth.

6) Regulations directly influence how the store is set up, how it does business, who it hires, some of the paperwork to be filled in, and a great deal more of its day-to-day decisions. Tax obligations are entered into the accounting system and dictate how transactions are handled, where some of the store's income is channeled, and so forth.

Finally, the business' processed information and material flow out of the retail store in many different ways. A typical store may deliver information or material in the following forms:

• Bank deposits of revenues.
• Payments to the landlord or mortgage holder and utilities.
• Purchase decisions and payments to product vendors.
• Advertising and other external communications.
• Answers and services to customers and potential customers, product purchases and deliveries.
• Tax returns and tax payments, as well as required reports to regulators.

Even if only in rudimentary form, all of this information or material processing activity should show up in the flow chart describing this retail store. To simplify your understanding of what is going on, mark the processes, operations and decision-making actions on the flow chart as boxes (you can use different shapes to indicate different types of processes), while the arrows between the boxes can be labeled—as necessary—with details about the information or material that's flowing. There may be many arrows to and from important boxes. It's a good idea to organize the chart so information or material tends to enter at one side of the paper, flow across the page, and leave on the opposite side. This way, when information or material is bottlenecked or poorly routed through the organization, the potential problem area shows up quite clearly on the flow chart.

Of course, flow charts for some businesses would be considerably more complex or include different processes than the one in figure 1. For example, a business that includes a manufacturing operation will require far more internal processing of raw materials into finished goods and shipping of completed orders than you normally find in retail operations. In a transportation company, tracking inbound and outbound packages and planning airline flights, train schedules, ocean voyages, trucking transfers, and other means used for transshipment, will be of primary concern. In a restaurant, "cooking" and "serving" processes will show up between the customer's ordering process and the "cashier" process.

There can also be a good deal of processing to handle personnel considerations. In almost every business, managers are concerned to some extent with planning and carrying out all the hiring and firing, training, promotions, pay increases, vacation scheduling, and internal job transfers that go on continually. As organizations become larger, personnel and other administrative functions take up more and more of the organization's time and effort.

REFINE THE INITIAL
ATTEMPTS AT A FLOW CHART

Don't expect to make a perfectly accurate flow chart in one attempt. Start with a single aspect of the business, such as money and finances, customers and service, manufacturing or products, or internal administration. Develop a rough approximation of how this one aspect of your business operates. Take a break, then go over the chart again to make sure you have identified all the inflows of information or material. Continue reworking the flow chart, each time concentrating on just one of the important aspects of your business. When you have all the parts properly charted, the picture will be very comprehensive.

To further refine the flow chart, trace each of these flows through the processes that follow, and revise the chart to more accurately reflect these sequences. Finally, continue charting each processing sequence until the information or material flows out of your business. Although even a rough chart is extremely helpful in streamlining and computerizing your operations, you can and should steadily refine the chart to reflect details of your business more accurately.

It's a good idea to let others in the organization review the flow chart and contribute their ideas, perceptions and suggestions. This is particularly true if these people must live with and/or implement the computerization decisions which the flow chart will guide. As with most other organizational activities, the more you ask people to contribute to the planning stage, the more effort and motivation they bring to completing their required tasks during implementation.

Since each business tends to be a unique expression of its owners, and of how it started and grew, no two businesses will yield identical flow charts. But this doesn't matter. All you need to be concerned about is making an accurate chart of your business, so you can streamline operations and automate the most important areas first.

Analyze the Flow Chart
When you have an accurate flow chart, go over it carefully. Look for:

- operations that can be combined effectively,
- processes that are redundant or unnecessary, or
- loops where information or material is processed more than once.

Combining operations tends to cut processing time and increase efficiency. Eliminating redundancies also saves time and expense. Although some loops can be desirable, straightening them out where you see no benefits is often a way to improve productivity.

For example, in a manufacturing business it's often productive for the number of units shipped each day to control the process of ordering raw materials or adjust the rate of manufacturing. A loop like this can be very helpful. In contrast, however, suppose the sales department processes all sales orders once to make sure pricing is correct, then sends them to manufacturing to receive an estimated delivery date, and then handles the orders a second time to schedule shipment dates. This should show up as a loop in the flow chart that carries no benefits and can profitably be eliminated.

In general, look to make the organization more efficient and responsive by combining, rearranging and perhaps eliminating processes to minimize delays and repetition. This kind of streamlining of day-to-day operations will greatly improve the flow of information or material through your organization whether or not you ultimately decide to install computers.

Apply Computer Capabilities to Important Business Activities
Assuming you have streamlined your organization, begin to look for places where computer capabilities can improve your most important business activities. Start by trying to identify which aspects of your business are most important to business success. Is it the quality of your final output? Is it a low price or specialized knowledge and skills? Is it the flexibility to deliver whatever the customer or client wants? Zero in on the critical parts of your business, and look for ways computers can be used to enhance or improve what you're already doing well.

You can also find targets for computerization by looking for time-consuming or expensive operations. Quantify how much time people spend on particular operations. Look at the most time-consuming ones to see if a computer might speed things up. Similarly, analyze the costs of particular operations, such as writing a check or a letter, or generating an invoice. If costs seem too high, investigate whether computerizing the process would save your business a worthwhile amount of money.

You can do more than just cut out waste, of course, because computers make it possible to add new processes that would be impossible or too costly to do by hand. For example, it takes a computer to do much in the way of sales analysis, performance projections, profit planning, or integration with customers and suppliers. But once you install computers and load them with the necessary business data, it becomes possible to start looking at which products are selling best and which worst, or which customers are providing the largest profits and which the least. It's also possible to begin projecting future performance and adjusting payroll, inventory, price or other levels to take advantage of anticipated demand. With spreadsheet software, you can easily examine a series of scenarios to determine the effect that possible changes to sales volume, pricing, product mix and other controllable variables might have on total profit.

Here is a brief rundown of the simplest, most effective ways to apply computer capabilities to the most important business operations and processes you have identified in your flow chart:

Information Storage and Retrieval

A great deal of business information processing consists of paperwork that people review, edit or copy and pass on to others. More and more organizations are finding ways to eliminate this paper and do the same processing on computer display screens instead.

Computer storage capacities are much greater than ever before, and in many cases far cheaper than the equivalent manual methods requiring paperwork, file folders, file cabinets or shelving. Depending upon your business' size and volume, you can realize savings in:

- processing speed,
- worker productivity,
- instantaneous transfer of work from one desk to another,
- smaller space requirements, and
- lower paper purchase and copying costs.

These savings can easily pay for the cost of the computer hardware, software, maintenance and training.

Companies are already using computers to store transaction and account information, and even to digitize the images of letters, invoices, checks and other items, eliminating the need to save the original documents. Medical records, as well other types of customer information and history are increasingly being stored in computers rather than file cabinets and heavy, cumbersome cardboard boxes. There are many more examples of the same basic conversion.

Information Entry and Computation

Computers originated as numerical computation machines, and they continue to excel at what today's computer users like to call "number crunching." As a result, virtually any business operation or process that involves numerical calculations is automatically a good candidate for computerization. Accounting is an obvious choice, as are cash register activities, sales analysis, order processing, inventory control and budget work.

For example, a typical business process involves entering items on a sales form, looking up the part numbers and prices, and then calculating the extensions, taxes and total. Computer systems can easily recognize the first few characters of a name or part number and automatically fill in the rest, greatly simplifying the entry of items on a sales form. In a flash, computers can look up and enter on the form part numbers and prices, and then automatically calculate the various subtotals and totals. Consequent reductions in labor requirements and human error normally result in significant savings.

The possibilities for automating are limited mainly by one's imagination. You can also automate other kinds of information processing. For example:

* in accounting systems a clerk can enter a transaction once and let the computer automatically post and distribute it to all the relevant journals; once the computer has calculated a series of financial ratios based on past performance figures, it can automatically calculate the same ratios on the numbers for any other period, as well;
* computer software can automatically schedule meetings and other appointments for a time when all those invited are available to attend;
* using "artificial intelligence," computer software can automatically apply the experience and knowledge of high-priced human experts to make recommendations to less-experienced employees regarding anything from loan application approvals to stress loading on an airplane wing.

Information Analysis, Manipulation
and Repetition with Word Processors
Information analysis, manipulation and repetition is very simple on computer systems. Word processing software, for example, lets you enter information at least as fast as you could print it on a typewriter. But once entered into word processing software, the text is available for easy analysis, manipulation and repetition.

You can use utility software to analyze the writing style, grade level or grammatical structure of the text. Or you can simply search through the text manually to see how many times you've repeated a word or a phrase. You can also verify that you've written enough about each of the various subtopics in a document.

You can easily copy or move parts of the text around, make global changes, find parts you want to review or change, adjust how it will print on the page, and print all or part of the text as often as you like. You can also "clip" parts of the computerized letter and use the text in other letters. By combining material from old letters with new ones, you can easily create entirely new documents.

Working with Electronic Spreadsheets
Electronic spreadsheets are much like word processors, but primarily for numbers. You can enter values into a spreadsheet about as fast as you can total them on an adding machine. But with an electronic spreadsheet, the values remain available for easy analysis, manipulation and repetition.

Analytical capabilities in utility or spreadsheet software allow you to check the relationships between various cells and formulas. You can also build a spreadsheet to analyze relationships between particular values or performance numbers. For example, it's easy to set up "discrepancy checking formulas" within an accounting spreadsheet that show at a glance if all the totals agree and balance out. You can easily copy or move some of the numbers around, combine them in different formulas, adjust how they will print on the page, and print all or part of the spreadsheet many times. You can also take some of the numbers and/or the results of various formulas and combine them with other numbers or results. By combining old numbers and formulas with newly entered information, you can create entirely new spreadsheets.

Working with Database Managers
Database management software gives you the power to manipulate and repeat both text and numbers. Once information is stored in a computerized database file, you can easily analyze, manipulate and repeat it.

For example, it's easy to print out a mailing list from a database of customer information. It's just as easy to do it again the following month, or to print just a portion of the mailing list for a special promotion any time. You can easily search for individual facts, and analyze a database of sales information for customer preferences and purchasing patterns, the performance of particular sales people, product acceptance by region or season, and much more.

The same kinds of analysis, manipulation and repetition are possible for information stored in other types of software, too.

Communications and Information Sharing

Computers are very adept at handling communications, whether between two or more separate computer systems or between people. Once sales data have been *scanned* or *punched* (see glossary) into a computer, for example, it's a relatively straightforward and instantaneous process to communicate some or all of that information to other computer systems for performing such business functions as accounting, billing and collections, or inventory management. Thus, instead of sending paperwork back and forth within your organization, it may be more efficient to punch or scan the data into a computer system, then make it available electronically to everyone who needs it.

Computers can also provide important services like electronic mail and file sharing or networking, that help people cooperate and coordinate to increase their effectiveness.

The computer-controlled transfer of files from one computer to another is called electronic mail. The files can contain any information, of course, but most often they're short memos, notes, inquiries, or other messages that traditionally would be in the form of interoffice mail, handwritten notes or quick verbal exchanges during a hallway meeting or a telephone call.

Unlike a meeting or a telephone call, however, e-mail does not require both parties to be available at the same time. So you can discover an e-mailed question from a colleague during the five minutes you have between morning meetings, give the answer, and get his reaction during another unexpected free minute toward the end of the day. Or at 4:30 on the West Coast you can draft an e-mail message asking for a price quote and send it to a sales manager traveling on the East Coast. When you get back to your office first thing the following morning, you're likely to find her e-mail reply waiting for you. The system can take or deliver messages any time of the day or night. It will hold a person's messages until asked for them, and can route your messages to whichever computer you happen to be using. Thus, you don't have to know where the sales manager is to communicate with her. You can also have the computer send the same message to any number of people.

Clearly, e-mail helps groups or teams keep in touch and coordinate their efforts, regardless of distance, heavy schedules or time zones.

Shared file services can effectively replace many copies of a letter, reference book, policy manual, report or other document. Instead of printing and distributing one copy to each person or each office, you store the material on a computer system where it is available to everyone authorized to read it, and also to those authorized to edit or update it. Aside from the considerable savings in paper and shipping costs, shared file services eliminate the logistical problems of keeping multiple copies of a single document. All changes are instantly available to everyone and the "old versions" are automatically replaced. And with shared file services, a whole work group or team can easily read the same materials and contribute to drafting a single document.

Computer communications can also bring far-flung offices into closer contact. Large data files can be transferred, people at regional centers can work with the home office database, and two or more computers can be linked to operate as one.

Personal Contact

Because computers are so quick at information storage and retrieval, they can be used to augment the kind of personal contact so important to sales, contract administration, client relations and other business operations. Specialized software packages exist to make this an extremely easy process to automate.

Software for personal contact is designed to access a database of names and other pertinent information, such as notes on previous conversations, promised follow-up activities, suggested dates and times to initiate the next contact, and so forth. Some software includes capabilities to set alarms and other reminders so you don't forget appointments.

By keeping this database up-to-date and referring to it often—particularly while talking on the phone or preparing for meetings—the software helps facilitate personal contact and eliminate problems of forgetfulness that can result in broken promises and poor relationships.

Computer Modeling and Simulation

If a mathematical formula, or a series of formulas, can adequately reflect how a business, a project or anything else operates, the computer is a perfect tool for building a "computer model" and rapidly evaluating what might be expected under specific conditions and eventualities. If the mathematical formulas become very complex, your "computer model" can be called a "simulation," and can sometimes be supplemented with visual, audio and other devices. Many computer simulations require massive amounts of processing power—far more than you can install on your desktop. But as technology continues to advance, the limits of what can be done with desktop or even portable computers steadily expand.

Many companies have saved thousands of dollars, and some even millions, by using computer models and simulations of car crashes, jet engines, bridge and building projects, new product launches, pricing changes, manufacturing processes, debt restructuring scenarios, direct mail advertising campaigns, and much more. Your business can probably benefit from using computers to model—and then optimize—some of its most important processes.

Graphics

Many people intuitively understand how to use and apply graphics in their day-to-day business operations. But for many others, graphics are a complex, less easily understood topic. To understand the world of computer graphics and its application to your business, you must first realize that there are three somewhat separate variations on fundamental computer graphics capabilities.

Business Graphics: Perhaps the most familiar aspect of computer graphics is business graphics—the standardized pie and bar charts that show numbers in visual form, as well as the simplified signs, slides, and other displays that add visual impact to ideas expressed in words and pictures. A great many software packages allow users to convert numeric values into a wide variety of charts. Various "presentation" programs combine business graphics features with the ability to make a carefully orchestrated presentation of these graphics either directly on the computer or by means of other media.

Image Capture and Manipulation: A second variation of computerized graphics capability is image capture, creation and manipulation. Here we apply computer speed and power to the full range of design, engineering and artistic work traditionally done by hand. For example, instead of airbrushing a photo—or any other image, for that matter—on his or her easel, an artist can now electronically airbrush it within the computer system. Similarly, a sketch, blueprint, circuit design, floor layout or any type of drawing can be completed within the computer. Most often these images are eventually printed on paper. But with very sophisticated design and engineering systems, the output can take the form of detailed manufacturing specifications or even coded instructions for computerized manufacturing equipment. At the high end, graphics programs evolve into Computer Aided Design (CAD), Computer Aided Engineering (CAE), and Computer Aided Manufacturing (CAM) software—subjects that are well beyond the scope of this book.

Electronic Charting: A third variation on computerized graphics capabilities automates the design, editing and printing of organizational charts and flow charts that previously had to be drawn by hand. Although this may seem to be just another form of artistic drawing, it's fundamentally a visual representation of text-based information. Computer software adds a new dimension of ease and power to this form of graphics by providing for rapid modification and "editing" of the information directly underlying the chart, and by letting the computer do the actual drawing automatically.

You should be aware that graphic software normally requires a more sophisticated and expensive computer monitor than nongraphic software. In addition, graphic output is nearly or entirely impossible to produce with a text-oriented *letter-quality* or *daisy-wheel* printer. Instead, graphic output requires a *laser* printer, a *dot-matrix* printer capable of printing graphics, or a *plotter*—a device for producing high quality graphic images, often on extra-large sheets of paper.

Design and Engineering Work: Modern computer aided systems for design, engineering and manufacturing have significantly cut the time and cost of product development. The hardware and software for these computer systems tend to be more powerful—and more expensive—than the general purpose systems you can use for simpler computer work. But the benefits and rewards can be proportionally larger, too.

Because these systems require a great deal of technical expertise—particularly if they are to be integrated with manufacturing or other business operations—guidelines for selecting and implementing them fall well outside the scope of this book. If you feel they may have value for your business, however, you should discuss your ideas and opportunities with experts in the appropriate areas of computer aided design, engineering or manufacturing.

If your needs are relatively simple, such as finalizing the floor plan of a new office or creating a graphic design, your general purpose computer—with the right software—can do a fine job.

Printing from Computers

A word processor is pretty useless if it can't print your documents on paper. Other applications, such as spreadsheets and graphic programs, also need at least occasional access to a computer printer. But in addition to these obvious printing jobs, computer printers can do a great deal more.

One chore that computer printing does extremely well is the rapid reprinting of a standard document. Suppose you have a letter that responds to a customer inquiry. Once it's saved in your word processing software, you can print a copy any time you need one to send out. Any information that is used as a standard, used for reference or just used frequently for any purpose is a good candidate for printing on computer. This can be far more efficient than having hundreds or thousands of copies duplicated all at once and storing them in a supply room or file cabinet where they take up valuable space, can get lost, damaged or forgotten, and become obsolete any time there is a change of phone number or mailing address.

Computer printing is also cost-effective for larger jobs. For example, your computer can print a batch of thousands of identical letters or flyers for a mass mailing, sometimes cheaper and nicer than you can have them commercially duplicated. By adding *mail merge* capability, your computer system can print the same basic letter any number of times, but include special, individualized information where appropriate on each copy, such as a name and address or the date of a customer's last purchase.

Another category of computerized output is "database printing." Here, software takes current information from a database, processes it through a formatting pattern or a "style sheet," and sends it to a printer. The result is a telephone directory, a citation list, a parts catalog, or any such document printed quickly, accurately and automatically. The main advantages are that large quantities of material can be formatted by the machine instead of the user, and whenever the data changes you can reprint the entire document automatically with full confidence that it contains the latest available information.

Computerized printing also supports the quick and inexpensive development of signs, presentation materials like slides for print or projection, and nicely formatted letters, memos, reports, proposals, brochures and other documents. If you wish, you can decide upon and computerize a universal "company style," and have the computer automatically print every item using the new arrangement.

HOW TO DECIDE WHICH
BUSINESS ACTIVITIES TO COMPUTERIZE FIRST

Most organizations have many opportunities to utilize computers. Unfortunately, you can't computerize them all at once. That's why it's important to prioritize and concentrate on the most important or potentially most profitable areas of work.

To do this, go over your flow chart and make a list of the best opportunities to use computers in your organization. Often, the most central operations are the best candidates for early consideration, and will probably yield large benefits when computerized. But the process of installing computers and getting them to work just right can be fraught with difficulties, so it's not wise to computerize too many central operations or processes at the same time. You could put your organization out of business before the first computer comes on-line. It's often safer to begin by computerizing a relatively isolated process that won't disturb other parts of the business if there are problems converting to an automated system.

Those areas that provide the most profit opportunity—where a bottleneck that prevents good service or better quality can be widened or where increased capacity can quickly remove a restraint on business growth—are also deserving of your attention.

In addition to looking for operations and processes you can computerize, it's often fruitful to work in reverse. That is, instead of looking for parts of your business that will benefit from computers, you consider which computer capabilities are most readily available to you, and then look for business operations and processes where you can apply these capabilities. You'll find it practical to get these applications running and start using them for whatever business operations and processes you can.

Two favorite applications for computers tend to be accounting and budgeting. They are well understood, isolated from other business operations, and perfectly suited to computerized number crunching.

Other computer capabilities, such as word processing and electronic spreadsheets, are particularly easy to implement. They are inexpensive and easily available from a variety of sources.

HOW TO INVESTIGATE AVAILABLE COMPUTER PRODUCTS

The process of acquiring computer systems for your business is simple and straightforward. It doesn't require very much time or computer expertise. We've already worked on how to identify business operations and processes that can be computerized, and how to improve and streamline them for greater efficiency before you take any steps toward computerization. Now it's time to review the available products—mostly "off the shelf" or readily available hardware and software packages, although theoretically you can review custom products or individual components, as well—and select those that best meet your needs. The factors to consider in your evaluation and selection process include:

- The quantity of data you will be processing.
- The sources for data input.
- The type and quality of output you will need.
- The need for various types of communications.
- The user's preferences or requirements for on-screen displays.
- The user's level of computer training / computer fluency.
- The available budget for installation, maintenance, and training.

The Quantity of Data You Will Be Processing
The quantity of data you will be processing will help weed out inadequate software packages. For example, a word processor may be limited to a 100-page document, and a database to 10,000 records. If your requirements exceed the software's limits, obviously you must look elsewhere.

But even where capacities seem sufficient, there can be differences. Some packages work fine for smaller quantities of data, but slow down considerably when asked to process larger amounts of data. Other packages are perfectly capable of handling millions or even billions of bytes at top processing speeds. In general, it's rare for software with large capacity to be unsuitable for handling smaller quantities of data. More often, it's a question of whether you can justify the higher cost of the more capacious software.

Hardware choices are also influenced by the quantity of data you will be processing. The older, less expensive computer designs are fine for simple word processing, and small database or spreadsheet files, but as the quantity of data goes up, these older processors, smaller memory capacities and slower hard disks fail to perform adequately. With hardware prices as low as they are, it's relatively inexpensive to buy a modern system capable of handling typical quantities of business data.

The Sources for Data Input

It's important to evaluate how well a particular software package can receive information from the sources you are likely to use. The main sources of data input are the keyboard, electronic file transfers and scanners.

Any software will probably be acceptable for keyboard input. However, some packages offer advanced capabilities—such as automatic duplication of previous input, or easily programmed keyboard macros— that simplify and speed up the data entry process. Electronic file transfers can be crucial for specific applications, and so you should be aware of your requirements and evaluate software very carefully against them.

Word processing, graphics and electronic spreadsheet software should be able to "read" or import a file, and "write" or export a file in the formats of other programs you may be using. Depending on the purposes for which you use these packages, you may or may not require such special transfer features as the ability to append information onto an existing data file, or to extract a portion of the information in an existing data file.

Since database software frequently contains and manipulates very large quantities of data, the ability to load data electronically into your database package can eliminate a great many hours of keyboard work. But to do this, the software must have the capability to receive transfers from your most important sources of information. The main consideration is whether the originating and receiving software (and sometimes hardware) can "translate" the data so it is directly and automatically usable.

You may also need special hardware—such as a *modem*, a *network* or a simple cable fitted between two computers—to make the electronic transfer possible. Simple electronic transfers are also done by carrying a floppy disk from one computer to the other, requiring only that both computers have compatible disk drives.

Scanners can be useful whether you need to load large quantities of paper-based information or just a single image into your computer. Many businesses use scanning to enter product codes at the point of purchase, at the receiving dock, and at inventory control checkpoints. Scanning can also be used to convert paper-based records to computer-based records that can be more easily processed and moved from one work station to another. The scanning process requires its own hardware, obviously, and some specialized software, which is either a separate application or a special capability included in other software. In evaluating scanning capabilities, consider how easily the software allows you to control the scanner hardware, and whether it provides scanning capabilities that meet your requirements. Also evaluate how well the software converts the scanned page into text, or into the exact image format your other applications can use.

The Type and Quality of Output You Will Need
Output requires hardware—a printer, a plotter, a display screen, a display projector, a fax machine, a speaker system or something else. But not all software works with all hardware, so check to make sure that the software you're considering and the output hardware you intend to use with it are compatible.

The simplest and most foolproof method for evaluating output is to try the complete system. Does the software do what you want with the hardware you'll provide for it? Although there's a great deal of technology underlying the compatibility issue, from your point of view it's mostly common sense: word processors should print good-looking letters on the printer you'll be connecting to your computer; graphics programs should print and display the way you want them to; multimedia systems should sound good and be loud enough with the speakers you'll be using. Don't even consider acquiring software until it can be satisfactorily demonstrated with the hardware you'll be using.

The Need for Various Types of Communications
Communications consists of computer-to-computer file exchanges, network exchanges, remote control compatibility, and facsimile transmissions.

A computer-to-computer file exchange can take place only after one computer connects to another. Generally this is done through a modem and telephone line, but you might use cables or other hardware. This allows you to send a file to a client's office, to copy a utility program from a computerized bulletin board, or to exchange data files or programs between your desktop computer and your laptop.

Network exchanges require a considerable amount of hardware and software to meet highly specific standards of compatibility. The computer, the associated network connections, the operating system, and application software must all be set up to work together or you may face serious problems. Application software that works great on a single computer may not work at all on a network, or may work but conflict with other software capabilities. Once a network is working properly and compatible software is loaded, users can share files, send and receive messages, transfer data files, and run application software residing elsewhere on the network.

Remote control software allows you to connect two computers—even over telephone lines—so they operate as one. Remote control capabilities are generally separate from other application software, and there are subtle issues of compatibility between application software and remote control software that must be satisfied for the computers to operate correctly. As always, test the complete hardware and software system you want to operate before you make any acquisition decisions.

Sending and receiving facsimiles (faxes) with your computer requires special hardware and software. In addition to communications features like those in your modem software, fax software must have access to Optical Character Recognition (OCR) capabilities—like those in scanner software—to convert the image file of a fax to and from a text file you can manipulate with a word processor, electronic spreadsheet or database.

The User's Preferences or Requirements for On-Screen Displays

The internal workings and performance capabilities of a computer's display screen must match those of the software you will be using. Otherwise, you may get a blank screen, or something less than what you expect.

Displays vary widely as to technology, overall screen size and pixel size (see glossary), number of colors they can display, and more. But there is a fair degree of standardization and, as a practical matter, you'll have only a few choices for computer display resolution and capabilities. The display system consists of the screen plus the hardware and software that control the screen, some of which must be installed inside the computer. Make sure all parts of the display system you acquire are compatible with each other and with any software you hope to utilize.

Software capable of beautiful graphics, for example, will operate poorly or not at all with a display screen designed only for text. Any software package can look great during the vendor's demo. But if your display doesn't meet the software requirements, it will look terrible (or fail entirely) on your office computer.

The User's Level of Computer Training/Computer Fluency
In a real sense, software is in the thick of the action where the user meets the computer. Many software packages—particularly statistical packages and electronic spreadsheets—have capabilities, intelligence, and preprogrammed operating sequences that go far beyond the average user's understanding and expertise. But this does not normally create a problem.

The real problem is when the software's commands, menu structure, or other aspects of its "human interface" are too demanding for the typical user. That is, you can't easily figure out what your choices are, what they mean, and how to select the one you want. Software written ten or more years ago, for example, normally had very primitive human interfaces that required the user to memorize command sequences and perhaps know something of computer programming languages. More modern interfaces assume the user has relatively little computer expertise. But software packages still vary greatly in their "ease of use," "user friendliness," or whatever term you prefer for this factor. So be sure to evaluate any software package to make sure it offers a human interface that you and others can accept, understand, and learn. Otherwise, the costs of overcoming resistances providing extensive training, and losing production time due to frequent operator errors may prove to be prohibitive.

The Available Budget for Installation, Maintenance and Training
I haven't spent much time discussing the costs of computerizing a business. One reason is that costs can vary from a few hundred dollars for a computer with simple word processing and electronic spreadsheet capabilities to highly sophisticated and advanced systems costing as much as you are willing to pay.

Sometimes more money will purchase a computer with significantly greater capabilities. For example, buying more data storage capacity or a slightly better display will let you run more powerful database and graphics programs. But you don't always get more results by spending more money. For example, acquiring a bigger, faster computer won't help much with word processing, where human thinking and typing speed are the major limitations on performance. But if you're computing the results of a complex simulation, a bigger, faster computer may cut the time required for processing by an hour or more.

In general, thought-intensive operations rarely go much faster when you upgrade from an adequate computer to the fastest-available system, but computer-intensive operations tend to finish more rapidly with faster processors, more memory, and larger storage systems.

EVALUATING COMPETING COMPUTER SYSTEMS

Before you can evaluate various computer systems for your organization, it's essential to establish definite functional requirements. In order to do that, you must decide precisely where in the business' flow of information and materials you intend to apply computer power, and exactly what function a computer will perform in each of these areas. Then you can begin to measure the abilities of available software against these requirements, and select the packages that best meet your needs. Finally, you can use cost and other performance criteria to decide what type and size of computer system you'll use to support the software you've selected. For example, you may want to use a single computer to handle several different business operations, one at a time, or many different computers—perhaps tied together in a network—to specialize in various business operations' or one larger computer to handle a series of business operations all at once.

Establish Functional Requirements

Obviously, each business will have its own set of computer opportunities and functional requirements. But let's suppose you decide to computerize accounting, sales and manufacturing, management and marketing operations within your business. Your functional requirements might specify that a computer system must:

- Process X number of accounting transactions each day.
- Store X number of accounting and client records of size Y.
- Retrieve any given accounting record within two seconds.
- Display and print sales and manufacturing statistics in the form of business graphics.
- Accept sales and shipping data already in your present sales order system, and export data to sales and manufacturing forecasting software (not yet acquired).
- Do word processing for reports and proposals, and generate printed materials suitable for marketing people to present to existing and prospective clients.

Evaluate Available Systems

With your functional requirements in hand, check with vendors, other businesses like yours, and perhaps consultants, to find software applications that might meet your needs. Focus on software first. As I already mentioned, it's more intelligent, practical and effective to let software decisions take precedence over hardware decisions (the only exception would be when you already have existing hardware that you wish to utilize more fully). Study the inputs (data handling requirements) and outputs (screen displays, printed reports, and other possibilities) of various software packages, trying to eliminate those that do not meet your functional requirements.

Test the applications that seem adequate. Use real data to see how well each one might operate as your business wants it to. No piece of software is likely to be perfect, so concentrate on finding the packages that most nearly fit your requirements and preferences.

Select Cost-Effective Software

On the basis of your results, select one or more software packages to acquire. Don't simply choose the top-selling software package in each category. Although these might meet your needs, there's at least a fair chance another package will do a better job for you. Instead, review several well-accepted packages with an eye toward their differences.

Set Hardware Requirements

When you've selected your software, use it as a basis to establish hardware requirements that will—in turn—help you choose the most cost-effective computer hardware on which to run the software. Buy 50 percent more capability than you feel you need right now, to allow for the future growth of your business and for computer uses you're not now envisioning.

HOW TO MANAGE THE TRANSITION FROM MANUAL TO AUTOMATED SYSTEMS

One of the most ticklish facets of computerizing your business is making the transition from manual to automatic systems. The brand-new computer system is likely to bring with it problems, inadequacies, software or hardware bugs that prevent proper operation, and other shortcomings. Employees may resist changing to the new system, and find fault with it—perhaps unreasonably. It may take weeks or months before the computerized system is operating as intended and people have become comfortable with it.

During this transitional phase, it's important not to abandon the old system too soon. Most organizations that computerize find it useful to run both systems for a while. This allows people to learn how to work the new computers and to verify that the computers come up with the same results as the established system they understand and trust. Keeping the old system fully operational also prevents loss of business or money due to start-up or break-in problems with the computerized system. Once the new system has established itself and people are comfortable with it, you can safely "cut over," or begin relying on it as your main production system.

3

Selecting Software

The natural inclination for novices who want to acquire a computer system is to put the cart before the horse. That is, they look at hardware first, and once the hardware is installed, they begin to look at software.

There are many good reasons why people make this mistake: hardware is often a large initial expense, and it is certainly a lot more obvious and impressive looking than software; often, a friend, relative or colleague will outgrow a computer and offer to let you buy, rent, or borrow it to "get you started"; and all the experts tend to talk about computer systems, rather than software systems, so it's natural to misunderstand the relative importance of hardware and software.

But all these reasons for putting the hardware before the software will lead you down the wrong path. Experience shows clearly that software is far more important than hardware. In most cases the computer does represent a large initial cash outlay, but with today's pricing structure, just purchasing your basic portfolio of useful application programs can easily run from 50 to 200 percent of the cost of the hardware itself.

Moreover, during the next few years you'll invest far more for the data your software contains than you'll ever spend for hardware and software combined. A big reason many people are fooled about the relative importance of hardware is that the cost of data is hidden. You generally don't write a check for it. But once you start working with the software, the cost of the time you—and perhaps others in your business—invest in learning how to operate the software will quickly dwarf the raw cost of the hardware alone.

Consider how much time—and therefore money—your organization will spend entering all the customer names and addresses, transaction details, operating results, and other data your computer will manage and manipulate. Consider how much *more* time the organization will commit to massaging that information into useful shape—sorting it, modifying it, studying and analyzing it both on the screen and in printed reports.

Clearly, your investment in software is far larger than your investment in computer hardware. And aside from money, there is another reason to emphasize software over hardware. To a very large extent, software determines what your computer system can and cannot do. Without software your computer is a near-useless pile of metal and plastic; with it, the system gains powerful capabilities. If you pick the right software, you should be able to quickly and easily perform all the data manipulations that are important to the future success of your business. But if you pick the wrong software, you may find that something crucial, such as adding a new client while entering sales orders or creating a chart automatically from the figures in your database program, simply is not possible.

In evaluating software, it's important to examine and understand every detail of what you expect to do with a particular package. Because each software capability is the result of many small, highly-detailed and intricately interlocking computer program statements, if a software package is not made to perform a particular manipulation, or if it is designed to handle only a certain number of items at one time, you're probably not going to be able to modify it. If a package shows any inadequacies or undesirable traits before you acquire and start using it, they will only become more glaring and inefficient afterwards. But even an adequate software package may not be good enough. Rather than start with a package that's adequate for now and hope to move smoothly to another package when your needs expand or change, you're far better off finding the package that meets both your present and your future needs.

OVERVIEW OF SOFTWARE CAPABILITIES

The smart approach to putting together a computer system is to find the software you want, and then buy the hardware required to support it. To help you, here's a brief overview of what to look for in any computer software, and also how to begin evaluating and selecting certain types of packages.

With all software, the main concern is that it operates in a way that makes sense to you or seems intuitive. There are many different ways to arrange command keystrokes, to organize computer processes and functions, and to display information on the computer screen. Some may be better than others, but the best package for you is the one most compatible with how you normally operate, and that best supports your organization's or staff's productivity.

Because computer procedures can become complex, in some situations there is a distinct advantage to software that provides on-screen menus of command options. The menus simplify learning to operate the software, particularly when people may not repeat the same computer operations for days, weeks or months at a time. However, some menu-driven software is slower to operate—and thus more frustrating—for people who already know the commands they plan to use. Ideally a software package will provide menus as well as a quicker means for the experienced person to bypass the slower menu system.

Data entry is by far the largest investment you'll make in your computerized database. For this reason, make sure the program allows for rapid data entry and simplified electronic transfer of information that is already computerized into the software you'll be using. One feature that makes for rapid data entry is a quick command keystroke that allows information previously entered to be instantly copied or repeated where you're currently working. When you're entering repetitive information, this "ibid" feature can save a great deal of time and prevent many typographical errors.

Another overall concern is the availability of help for users who "get stuck" or lose their way. On-line help—if clear, accurate and sufficient—is often better than printed instruction manuals, because it's usually faster and easier to read directions from the computer screen in front of you than to get up from your desk, search bookshelves and file drawers for the proper manual, and then find the page you need. Context-sensitive help is the easiest form of on-line help because the computer automatically presents information about the software's current operation or status. That is, if you select "Help" while you are entering data, the context-sensitive on-line help system will begin by displaying information about data entry. This allows you to start working with the software almost immediately and to learn what you need as you go along.

A software capability that's very important is immediate data correction. In some programs, correcting an error is a cumbersome process. In others, it's a simple matter of backspacing or moving the cursor to the error and typing the new information to replace the old.

Some software—particularly special purpose or customized software—does not provide such immediate and direct data-correction capabilities. For example, you may not be able to move the cursor back until the entire screen is filled in, or moving backward to correct an error may unavoidably erase everything the cursor passes over. Software that allows a person to correct his or her mistakes easily, quickly and immediately tends to make people far more productive than software that does not. Although some data entry errors won't be noticed and must be caught by other error-correction techniques, over the years immediate corrections have proven to be the fastest, easiest and least expensive means of keeping data accurate.

A major issue for software selection involves electronic networking. In many organizations, two or more computers are linked together to form a data-sharing network. One advantage of networking is that a single copy of application software and data files can be used by all the computers on the network. Buying one copy for a network is usually less expensive than buying many copies for many computers, and of course the one copy is easier to modify and update. For software to operate over a network, though, it must be written for the specific network you are using. So before you buy software intended for use on a network, make sure it is compatible with your network hardware and software. If not, the package can refuse to run, or run only on the computers where it resides.

In order to avoid future software roadblocks or dead ends, always choose software that provides a means of converting your data files into a standardized, simplified arrangement of text and numerical characters without any of the vendor's proprietary "control codes." In most cases, these so-called "ASCII" files can then be read by new, different, or more powerful software packages with a minimum of re-keying.

The Accounting System

Accounting is a complicated activity, and it can take a great many hours of work to record information and maintain accurate books. But as you know by now, computers can do this sort of detail work much faster and easier than you can do it by hand. That's why computerized accounting is quite often the single application that causes a business to install a computer system. In many other situations, an accounting application helps cost-justify a computer system desired for some other purpose. For whatever reasons, accounting is one of the business operations most frequently computerized.

Because there is so much demand from so many different types and sizes of organizations eager to install accounting software, commercial software publishers market literally hundreds of accounting packages. Since handling the complexities of accounting calls for a large amount of computer code, many accounting packages are written in separate "modules," each one providing some specific accounting functions. This makes programming easier and also holds down software prices by allowing people to buy only as much accounting capability as they want and need. However, the inherent complexity of accounting software means that finding the best accounting application for your organization can be time-consuming and difficult. In most situations, you should forget your quest for "the best" and settle—with much less time and effort invested—for a proven accounting package that meets your minimum requirements. If you've chosen well, you can always upgrade later on.

This book does not discuss how to do accounting, nor does it describe particular accounting functions or procedures. Instead, it details the issues that should concern you about the overall operation of the accounting system you evaluate. Then it covers important issues in each of the accounting areas you may want the system to handle. I have associated these areas with specific functions, but the accounting packages you investigate may well cluster these functions somewhat differently. Don't be too concerned about which functions are grouped together. Simply consider and compare each function individually, and then buy the program that offers the best combination and arrangement of the functions you need and want.

If you know little or nothing about accounting, you shouldn't be selecting your business' accounting package. Pay an expert, and take his or her advice. If you do understand accounting, here is how to transfer what you know to computerized accounting systems.

Overall Issues for Accounting Software
A fundamental attribute of accounting software is its information handling capacity. For example, to help structure and control the flow of orders, inventory, income and expenditures many business operations are structured as several different companies, and/or use several different bank accounts. Clearly, the accounting system you select must be able to support the number of companies and accounts you require, as well as the number of monthly transactions you conduct.

Although it seems a technical issue, the number of times the data itself is stored is also important. Think conceptually for a moment. Some accounting programs store a piece of information—whether a transaction amount, a vendor name or an amount due—in one and only one place. The information may show up in many different screens, but it is always stored in and retrieved from a single file location. The advantage of storing a single piece of data in a single place is that changes are easy to make, and computer storage space is utilized more efficiently.

But other accounting packages take a different conceptual approach. They store a single piece of information in two or more locations. For example, a customer name may be stored once in an accounts receivable module, and again in a sales analysis or sales tracking module. If the software takes care of copying information automatically from one location to another, and you're not storing megabytes of information, there may be no practical difference in these two information-storage strategies from the user's point of view. However, software that stores the same information in several different locations can require that you enter the information many times. Storing the same information many times can take longer and create more opportunities for error, and can lead to problems if the software does not simultaneously update all the corresponding storage locations to reflect a change. For example, you could update a customer's telephone number in the accounts receivable module, but leave the general ledger module unaware of the update. You could then pull up the wrong phone number, or a computer process could inadvertently copy the old number from the general ledger to the accounts receivable module, effectively wiping out the update. Or the two modules may not recognize that the two entries are meant to be identical, and will not correctly merge or consolidate the data for this customer. If you have ever received two separate bills for the same product or service, you've experienced these kinds of problems.

Another overall concern is the ability of the software to allow for many different entries to be associated with a single transaction. Individual accounting transactions will normally involve several different invoices, products, purchase orders, or credit memos. Sophisticated accounting software therefore allows a $50 payment from a customer, for example, to be allocated toward several different outstanding invoices, or allows several partial payments to be allocated toward a single invoice, and so forth.

One characteristic of accounting is that many entries are repetitive. For example, every customer will pay the same amount for the purchase of a standard product, or a particular customer will make the same purchase every week or every month. Similarly, payroll checks will be made out to the same names every week, and the same vendors will be paid every month. To save time, many accounting packages provide for automatic entry or retrieval of such recurring information. The software can offer the information through an on-screen menu, or it can simply "fill in" the rest of the entry as soon as it recognizes a name, word, price or other entry. For example, if you enter the letter S under "customer's name," the computer may immediately offer "Sears Roebuck & Co." from your list of established customers. If the list contains two customers beginning with S, the computer may wait until you enter a second character before offering a name. There are many different ways to provide automatic data entry. Any of them can be a great convenience and time saver. Some may work better than others for your particular needs.

A related consideration is the availability of "batch" as well as "individual" transaction processing. Obviously, an individual transaction would be one order, one check, one invoice or any other single item. A "batch" process would involve more than one, perhaps thousands of similar transactions. For example, at the end of the week you can do the payroll individually, so that under your direct control the computer calculates and prints each check, or you can "run" the weekly payroll as a "batch" (or a "batch process"), so that the computer calculates and prints all the payroll checks automatically while you remain free to do something else. Some accounting systems offer batch processing capabilities, others do not. Whether or not you want this depends on your organization, and on how you will be using the system.

Because software is simply a collection of separate functions, skillful programmers can write software with any structure they desire and make it perform accounting functions in any desired combination or arrangement. Make sure the software in which you will invest so much time and data meets your organization's needs in the most practical sense: it must do the work you want done in the way that best supports your business. If you find yourself changing years of business practice to conform to an arbitrary arrangement of software functions, you're probably moving in the wrong direction.

Finally, some accounting packages have extra "bells and whistles," such as a built-in calendar or calculator, fancy printed reports or screen designs, and advanced capabilities you probably won't use in your business. These may be worthwhile features. But if they do not help you with your day-to-day accounting and are not important to you for other reasons, don't be blinded by them and mistakenly acquire application software that does an unsatisfactory job on the truly important tasks.

The General Ledger

The General Ledger (GL) is at the heart of every set of accounting books. When accounting becomes computerized, the GL often becomes the central module in the software package. In simple checkbook-balancing programs, the GL may be the whole accounting package.

Within the GL will be your Chart of Accounts. This is an organized listing of category names and associated reference numbers you can attach to each transaction. You can also list those to whom you make payments and those who pay money into your business. With a paper-based accounting system, you can always staple another sheet of paper onto the back of your Chart of Accounts to make room for more. But with software, the system is designed and written for a maximum number of entries. Before you acquire an accounting application, make sure there is enough room in the Chart of Accounts for all the identifying categories you are likely to require in the next three to five years.

While you're checking capacities, make sure the system can keep track of enough transactions for each accounting period. Each transaction will be a payment or partial payment, a transfer from one account to another, a check you write, a bank deposit, and—depending on how the software is designed—possibly orders, shipments sent and received, interest payments credited or paid out, and much more. If you ever have more transactions than the software can handle, you'll simply be out of luck.

Depending upon your finances and how you operate, you may want your GL software to track a number of credit cards, checking and savings accounts, and various loans. Make sure it has the capacities you want in these areas, too.

You will certainly want the GL to deliver automated reports, such as a monthly Trial Balance, an Income Statement and Balance Sheet, and year-to-date figures, as well as summaries of liabilities, income and expenses. You may also want the GL to support budget planning and to report on actual versus budgeted expenses for each accounting period. But not all systems offer all these reports and capabilities, and of those that do, some are more powerful and easier to use than others.

Once you move beyond a system that's self-contained, or you begin to need capabilities more extensive than those of a General Ledger module, you'll want to add other modules to provide more sophisticated accounting features, such as Accounts Payable (AP).

The Accounts Payable Module

Obviously, this module is designed to track all the payments you're obligated to make. Begin your evaluation of an AP module by making sure it has enough capacity for the number of vendors you'll be paying, and for the number of invoices you'll be receiving for payment each month. Also, it might be wise to favor AP software that can print or display a statement of your past and present activities with a single vendor, as well as a schedule of upcoming bills and their due dates. Some AP packages have the ability to capture each vendor's discount schedule and compare this against your due dates to recommend a payment date that maximizes your cash flow while minimizing net carrying charges.

When the GL is specialized enough or your accounting requirements are broad enough to need support from an AP module, you'll almost always need an Accounts Receivable (AR) module, as well.

The Accounts Receivable Module

This module is designed to track all the invoices you generate and send out, and allocate payments as you receive them. Make sure any AR module you acquire has enough capacity for the number of customers and others who will be paying you, and to track the number of invoices you'll be issuing each month.

Depending on how your operations are organized, you may want your AR package to have specific capabilities for handling cash receipts, as well as checks, credit cards, and electronic funds transfers of various types. For many business organizations, no sale is ever made without some negotiation of terms. Others sell everything at standard prices. If terms of sale vary greatly from one transaction to another, your AR package should be able to record the actual price of a product or service out the door. Since many customers do not pay in full on time, your AR package should also record partial payments against invoices. You may also want the software to keep track of the sales person responsible for each transaction.

It's often important for an AR package to generate complete statements for specific customers, or to reprint historical invoices (to replace a missing one requested by a customer, for example). You may also want to see aging reports, past due invoices, and cash flow forecasts based on existing receivables. Not all software can do this easily (or at all).

The Sales Analysis Module
The various functions of Sales Analysis (SA) are often built into other modules of the accounting system. But however they are organized in the software, it's useful to be able to generate reports based on sales data. For example, you may want to examine the sales of a particular sales person or a particular product. You may want to compare the sales of various products from one period to another—say week by week, month by month, or season by season. You may also want to see how sales volume has responded to recent or historical pricing changes.

With some software, certain sales analyses are available with just a few keystrokes, while others are entirely beyond the capacity of the system. With more flexible software packages, you may be able to generate virtually any sales analysis you desire. Flexibility is useful if you do not know in advance exactly what data you want to analyze, or what comparisons you want to examine. However, some of this flexible software requires specific programming skills and a good understanding of computer processes before a new or complex report will issue forth from the printer.

A happy medium between these extremes is software that provides flexibility to add new reports, but has the capacity to "automate" the command sequences required to produce reports that are more familiar and commonly required.

The Payroll Module
Not every business needs a Payroll Module (PM), but converting to one and using it can make the weekly payroll and payroll tax routines a lot faster and simpler to do. As with other modules, make sure the PM has enough capacity for the number of employees, the number of payroll checks, and the types and kinds of payroll taxes you are required to pay. It should offer automated functions to do all the required local, state and

federal withholding calculations and accounting procedures, including an adjustable table of values to tell it when the maximum amounts have been withheld. It's also good if the PM can print the W-2 and 1099 forms you're required to give your employees and independent contractors.

You should also ensure that the PM will print checks and payroll stubs in the right size and format for your purposes. For example, you may need to itemize on the checks or stubs the number of hours worked, regular and overtime, and the hourly rate for each. There may also be checks of a certain size and style on which you will want the system to print. Specific software packages may or may not be flexible enough to do the printing the way you want it done.

Depending on your business, you may want the payroll system to account for tips, and for 401(k) plan deductions and any matching contributions you make. For complicated situations, the payroll system should have provisions that make it easy to adjust, calculate and perform all the various deductions your payroll may require, including—if necessary—commissions.

Although not strictly a payroll function, PM software (or another module, perhaps one for personnel) can keep track of vacation and sick leave, and make adjustments to paychecks to reflect days not worked during a particular pay period.

The Point of Sale/Invoice Writing Module
Today's personal computers can also serve as a cash register. If used in this way, it's easy and valuable to add a Point of Sale (POS) and/or an Invoice Writing (IW) module that automates most or all of these sales-related functions.

As with other modules, make sure the POS/IW software has enough capacity for the number of transactions you're likely to enter during each day and/or accounting period. It should be able to refer to a complete price list for each transaction, and calculate or look up the variable pricing that might apply (such as quantity discounts or contracts with certain customers for special pricing). If the computer is printing sales receipts or invoices, it should automatically calculate the extension (item price times quantity sold), add applicable sales tax, and total the purchase.

The POS functions should include cash drawer control, capacity for multiple sales people using one cash drawer or one computer cash register, and quick quotes on items when customers request price information. If your business tags items with bar codes, it saves time and improves accuracy to have the computer scan the codes at the register, print the sales receipt and automatically note the items sold for deduction from inventory listings.

The IW software should not only enable the computer to print a numbered invoice or sales receipt, it should print packing lists and work orders, as necessary, to fulfill invoices. If you don't have an AR module, the IW module should be able to print a list of past-due invoices.

The Inventory/Purchase Order Module

The Inventory/Purchase Order module (IPO) is very useful where inventory management provides important opportunities for profit enhancement. The IPO should provide instant access to stock-on-hand detail, as well as part numbers and vendor information. It should track usage of inventoried items, and automatically provide a warning when stock-on-hand drops to a preset level where a reorder must be issued to prevent stock from running out.

Whether the IPO or the AP module actually prints purchase orders, it's important for the accounting software to coordinate purchases with each vendor's discount schedule to recommend order quantities and reorder intervals that provide minimum pricing on long-term purchase agreements.

Once a purchase order is issued, the IPO module should track anticipated delivery dates and provide a warning if any shipment is not received on time. Some IPO modules have full-blown "just in time" capabilities to track usage of supplies and raw materials on an hourly or daily basis and to issue frequent orders—sometimes electronically—to regular vendors.

A good IPO module will also provide vendor reports regarding current and past orders. These reports will specify the average number of days from order to delivery, and will indicate the vendor's on-time performance. For inventory management, the IPO should provide valuation reports, and should print tags, labels, and whatever forms you may need for warehouse/parts department controls.

Other Accounting Modules

Within more general accounting packages, there are sometimes highly specialized modules to perform such specific functions as fixed asset management, capital management and contract management. You may want to investigate the availability of special-purpose accounting packages and modules that will enable your computer system to enhance your ability to do business profitably. For certain industries and large-scale organizations, there are highly specialized accounting packages designed to run an entire business.

The Database

A database program, or database manager, is essentially a software tool for storing, manipulating and retrieving information. There are two reasons why this is an invaluable computer capability for business. First, it provides a powerful "memory" so that virtually any amount of information on any topic—from customer names and buying habits to listings and descriptions of the millions of parts that make up the space shuttle—can be searched in the wink of an eye. Second, the database manager provides a powerful tool for analyzing the information, for looking at trends and patterns, and perhaps even for forecasting what will happen next. By examining customer buying habits over the past seven years, for example, you may be able to project how much of which products-they will buy in the coming year.

The first step in obtaining the benefits of a database application in your business, of course, is to select the database software that meets your specific needs for capacity, capability and speed. A few database programs are "free-form." That is, you can put any text or numerical information—in some cases even images or sounds—into the database and retrieve it again later piece by piece. Over the years, however, free-form database programs have usually proven useful only for very special purposes where it's difficult to know which "key words" will be used for searching and retrieving the information in the database.

Most database software takes a more structured approach, organizing the information fairly strictly into records and fields. These "structured" database programs are the most widely available and generally useful, by far, and are the only database programs we will discuss here. To understand how a structured database program operates, visualize the registration desk of an old hotel. Behind the desk is a wall of pigeonholes, one for each room, into which the clerk puts room keys and messages for the guests. The entire wall of pigeonholes constitutes our structured database. In our example, each row of pigeonholes represents a whole floor of the hotel. Each column of pigeonholes represents the same room on each floor. Thus the bottom-left pigeonhole is room 101, the first room on the first floor. The top-left pigeon hole is room 1001, the first room on the tenth floor. The database software in our example is the desk clerk who knows where to put things in and find them again for retrieval.

If this pigeonhole system were computerized, each row would be called a "record." Each pigeonhole, and each column of pigeonholes, would be called a "field." Whether you have ten records in your database, or ten million, the first field in every record contains the same class or category of information.

For example, in a mailing list database, each full record represents a person. The person's first name would be stored in the first field, and his or her last name would be stored in the second field. The third field might hold the person's street address, the fourth field the city, the fifth field the state, and the sixth field the ZIP code. Check any record in the database and you will see that the first field contains a first name, the second field a last name, and so forth. (You could separate everything into fewer fields, of course, but then you'd sacrifice some of the power of the database to manipulate and manage the information.)

This arrangement of fields (sequence, size and type of information) is called the "file structure" of the database. For technical reasons, you can and should specify a "type" of data for each field. The most common data "type" specifications are: "alphanumeric" for letters and numeric characters (such as 451 South Main Street); "numeric" for numbers you'll want to add or multiply (such as 23 or 3,678); "date" for calendar dates; and in some database software "financial" for dollar figures. With some database software, "alphanumeric" fields also require a size. That is, the software wants to know how many characters you may place in this field. With good software you can always change the field size; of course, if you reduce the size of a field you will be discarding any excess information it already contains.

With most good database software, the details of the file structure do not interfere with your ability to arrange how you look at the information. The structure merely provides the software with internal references and shortcuts so that when you have 10,000 records, it can still find and display any name you want within a few seconds, which is far faster than a comparable search in a free-form database.

Now let's examine some of the things you can do with a structured database program and how to decide which one you should acquire.

Data Entry

There are basically only two ways to enter information into your database. You (or someone else) can manually type the data into your computer at your keyboard, while the software receives this information sequentially and places each piece into the next available field and record of your database file, or you can arrange information already inside a computer so it follows the proper electronic structure for your database software, and then have the software electronically "read" the information sequentially and place each of the items into the next available field and record of your database file.

Information you enter manually can come from a printed list, handwritten notes, dictation or any other source. If you want to build a customer database, for example, you might enter your first 100 customers all at once from previous listings, then add one new customer a week as they come in and buy.

Information the software reads electronically will come from one or more existing computerized lists. It's quite common to write information out of one database program into an electronic file where it can be read by a new, more powerful database program. This is a simple, fast process, provided both your old and new database software can read and write the same types of files, such as standard ASCII format files, or provided that at least your new database program can read and write the old one's files.

Once you have placed information into a database file, you can always edit it. So if you happen to place records out of sequence, you can easily sort them or otherwise modify the file to meet your needs. Sequence is important only when first entering information, and only because the computer is orderly enough to want to complete all the fields in record 1 before it starts with the first field in record 2, and so on.

View/Browse

This software function allows you to read the information already in your database. In a sense, it's like simply asking the computer to show you everything in the file. You'll want to view/browse your data for two main reasons: to check the facts already in the file, and to see what the information in your file generally "looks like." When you have more specific reasons to look through the file, you'll use the "ask/select/query" function discussed a bit later in this section.

Most database programs show you a file in the arrangement that you originally created it. That is, if you specified a size of ten characters for the first field, it shows up as being ten characters long when you view the file. But for specific applications, you may want to see only the first four of these ten characters. At some point, you may also decide that you want to view the first, seventh, and eighth fields, but none of the others. You may want all the fields of a single record to show up on the display screen at once, or you may prefer to have the first two fields of twenty-five different records on the display at one time.

Making any of these changes depends on the application software having the necessary capabilities. Some only permit a single view of the data. Others permit different views, but only one at a time. Other software will allow you to "store" several views of the data, and switch from one to the other very rapidly. Check out the capabilities of the database software you are considering, and make sure it gives you the viewing flexibility you desire before you acquire it.

Ask/Select/Query

Every time you have a specific question about what's in your database file, you rely on the software's "ask/select/query" function. Technically, it's always a "query," but some software packages use the word *ask* or *select* to mean the same thing. For convenience, we'll call it an ASQ.

There are many different ways to ASQ a database file. At the most sophisticated level, programmers are struggling to develop "natural language" capacity so you can talk to your computer the way characters in science fiction movies talk to theirs. Although amazing strides are being made, we're not in the future yet. Before you acquire a database program, go over its ASQ function in some detail. Enter sample data and try to ASQ it to provide the kind of information you'll want from the production system on which your business will rely. Specifically, determine whether a complex ASQ can be stored on disk and later retrieved for reuse. If so, you can develop standard ASQs and recall them later by name or number without remembering the details of how each one was constructed or how it operates. Also determine whether ASQs can be edited. If so, you can start with a simple (or an incorrect) ASQ and modify it progressively until it produces the information you seek.

As you select a database program, consider its capacity to handle larger and larger files. Some programs are strictly limited in the number of records, the number of fields, and even the size of fields they can handle. Even though a program's capacity seems large enough for your present needs, ASQ performance in extracting the information from a large database may still be much slower than the same ASQ on a smaller database. Do some tests or obtain expert opinions to determine how well the software will perform with the kind and quantity of data you intend to use.

Another concern is whether the database is capable of working with just one data file at a time (a so-called "flat file" database program), or with more than one (a so-called "relational" database program). Relational database programs offer more power and flexibility, and often eliminate the need to store the same information in several different files. But the more sophisticated uses possible with a relational database program may be more difficult to understand and learn.

A feature available in some software is the ability to "index" data. The index may also be called a "key field" or a "query speedup." Essentially, however, an index to the data allows the software to find what you are looking for more rapidly. Some software builds an index to the first field in the record automatically, others build an index only on command. Some can index only a single field, others can index as many fields as you wish. Searches are faster only within the indexed fields. Compare the capabilities of the software to your requirements as you decide which package to acquire.

Data Copy, Data Add, Data Subtract
These data manipulation functions are called many different things by many different database programs, but they boil down to copying to and deleting from data files. "Data copy" is the ability to make a duplicate of a specific data file. "Data add" is the ability to copy data from one data file into another. "Data subtract" is the ability to remove from one data file the specific information contained in another data file.

As you work with your data, you will have frequent reason to apply these three functions. So before you acquire database application software, make sure they are relatively quick and easy to use.

Design, Print, or View Reports (with Computations)
The power of your database software to generate reports on the data it contains is central to making full use of this information. Think of a report as an ASQ, but far more elaborate. A report may be printed on paper, may be displayed on the computer screen, or may be saved into a file on disk. The report may simply list some or all of the data in the database file. For example, a report generated by a database program may list 50 records from the data file that meet certain specifications— all sales of more than $1,000 in January, for example. Or the report may describe the number of records and the field sizes contained in the data file. This is useful for keeping track of the kind and quantity of information stored in a large data file.

But many of the most useful reports actually calculate new information not literally contained in the database file. For example, if a data file contains the records of each sale, the database software should be able to generate a report showing the total sales for a specific period of time. It should also be able to calculate the average price of the products sold, and it should be able to provide a list of the 100 customers who spent the most money during a given period. It may also be able to calculate which customers have the lowest ratio of shipping costs to total purchase amount, or any other ratio you may want to examine.

Different databases will generate these kinds of reports in different ways. Before you acquire a database, make sure it operates in a way that makes sense to you. The reports you want should be easy to generate. It should be straightforward to specify exactly what calculations on data you want and (does it go without saying?) they should be mathematically accurate.

Give some thought to how you want the report presented. You'll probably want critical reports to be printed on paper for distribution and/or review by several people. But many reports can be viewed on the screen and discarded without going all the way to hard copy. In some cases, you may want to save a report in a computer file, and either view it on the screen or incorporate some or all of it into a word processing document or electronic spreadsheet. Make sure the software you select has the capability to deliver the information you want in the form you want it.

It's also advantageous if the commands required to generate a report—the "report specification"—can be saved to disk and used again.

This allows people who don't know the details of operating the computer software to generate reports designed by those who do.

Change Structure, Field Size and Data Type

This is a relatively esoteric and technical detail of database application software with which most end users needn't concern themselves. Simply be aware of the capabilities of database application software to make changes in file structure, particularly the number and order of fields, and the size and data type of existing fields. Depending on the software, some changes are possible at any time, some changes are possible but may delete some of the existing data in the fields you change, and some changes may be impossible.

If you are choosing between otherwise equivalent packages, favor the software with the greatest flexibility in this area. It's particularly important that you be able to add fields at any time. It's also useful if you can change the size of existing fields (making them larger shouldn't result in the loss of any data). This flexibility allows your computer system to evolve from time to time, changing your present data file structure to a different one that will be more useful in the future. It also means you don't have to anticipate every possible requirement down the road. You can simply start using your database program, and make changes to your data file structures as they occur to you or as they become necessary. Experience shows that this flexibility is a welcome luxury for most business situations.

Data Import/Export

We touched on this briefly under data entry, above. Data import/export refers to the capability of the software to read other programs' data files into its own data file format, and to write the information from its own data files in the file formats of other programs.

Good data import capabilities allow you to use your new database software with information from other programs, most importantly your previous database software. Good data export capabilities allow you to use your data in other programs, and virtually guarantee that your data will not be trapped in the present software format, but can easily be made available to more advanced database software you may acquire in the future.

Programming Language and Macros
Database operations can become complex, tedious and time-consuming. To get the information you want may require half a dozen—or dozens— of separate computer commands, operations, and interim results. Moreover, when you set your database software to work on thousands, tens of thousands, or hundreds of thousands of records, it can take hours to search, sort, compare and calculate the information you want in your report.

You can type in the instructions to do all this yourself, if you like, giv- ing the required software commands at the proper time and in the proper sequence. Or, you can simply "program" the software to do a series of complex, tedious, and time-consuming operations at the press of a few buttons. There are two basic ways to accomplish this programming with database applications. You can use a "programming language" built into the software, or a "macro" capability that is either built into the software or provided by special-purpose "keyboard utility" software that runs on the computer at the same time as the database software.

Either way, you—or someone skilled in programming techniques— sets up a series of command sequences, menus, and possibly display screens to simplify the process of commanding the software to accom- plish the ordinary tasks for which it is used. This is neither the time nor the place to cover database programming languages in any detail, but you may want to consider the power as well as the difficulties of using the programming language in any database software you consider for acquisition.

The Electronic Spreadsheet
Electronic spreadsheet software is one of the most important and valu- able computer products you can use in business. In the guise of Visicalc, and later Lotus 1-2-3, the first electronic spreadsheets were responsible for moving personal computers out of the garages and workshops of hobbyists and onto the desk tops of corporate executives. The reason is simple: this computerized version of the time-honored accounting spreadsheet is virtually as simple to set up and use as the traditional paper-and-pencil variety. But there's a major difference. Once you've got it set up, the electronic spreadsheet instantly applies all the power of the computer to what is otherwise a very tedious and time-consuming activity—actually performing all the mathematical calculations written

onto the spreadsheet. What's more, as you change the numbers and/or the mathematical formulas, the software instantly recalculates the entire spreadsheet and shows you a new set of results.

If you've used electronic spreadsheets, you can skip the following section, but if you're unsure about what they are or how they work, pay attention.

How an Electronic Spreadsheet Works
Visualize a large piece of paper ruled into vertical columns and horizontal rows—a standard accounting spreadsheet. On this paper spreadsheet you pencil in the names of some items and their associated costs. For example, paper, $1.00, pencils, $0.50. Now you manually add up the individual items you've just written down. In this example, your total for paper and pencils is $1.50.

The computerized spreadsheet is analogous to the paper one: you type in a label, and next to it (in the same row, next column), a figure. The difference is that when you finish your entries, you don't manually do the math. Instead, you enter a "formula" in the column and row location (called a "cell") where you want the column total to be. The formula is a mathematical statement like the kind used in equations. You enter the formula, and the computer automatically evaluates it and displays the "answer."

You can enter an infinite variety of possible formulas. In this example you want to know the sum of your other entries, so you enter a formula that refers the computer to the cells you designate, and tells it to add up all the numbers it finds in them. The computer immediately calculates the results, just the way you did by hand. Its result: paper and pencils, $1.50. The most important difference between the computerized spreadsheet and the paper-based manual one is this automatic calculation of results.

Instead of entering a formula that refers to other cell locations, you could have typed in a formula containing the actual cost figures to be totaled. Although this works, it seriously weakens the software's innate flexibility to accept changes later on. When you use cell references as much as possible, the computer stands ready to recalculate any values that may appear in those cells.

As you can imagine, and as I'll explain in later sections, this combination of formulas, cell references, and instant recalculation puts tremendous computing power literally at your fingertips. In fact, the use of a formula containing cell locations rather than specific numbers turns out to be central to the effectiveness of the electronic spreadsheet. In our example, as soon as you change the cost of any item in your list, or you add more items (say, paper clips at $0.25), the formula you've written in the "column total" cell instantly causes the computer to recalculate the new numbers you've entered and to display the new, updated answers.

Beyond simple addition of numbers, spreadsheets offer about a hundred formulas for instant financial, trigonometric, mathematical, statistical and other computations. In addition, you can enter any formula you wish—subject to certain rules and guidelines—and the software will instantly compute the results for you. Aside from mathematical capabilities, modern spreadsheet software offers additional features, such as business graphics, simple database capabilities, extensive formatting of printed spreadsheets, and automatic linkage of spreadsheet information to word processing documents. Taken as a whole, electronic spreadsheet software offers a very simple route to sophisticated computer power.

Uses of Electronic Spreadsheet Software
Electronic spreadsheet software is popular not only because it's powerful, but because its power is generic enough to be used for countless different purposes. Building on the basic math capabilities of electronic spreadsheets, it's possible to accomplish quite a wide range of work with this one type of software.

Computer Models
The electronic spreadsheet is ideal for creating mathematical models of business operations—real or proposed. Whether you're discussing a retail store, a commercial building, a multilevel marketing program, a manufacturing operation or anything else that can be described with numbers, the electronic spreadsheet is a simple, powerful tool for quickly building an accurate mathematical model of any business operation.

For example, if you're manufacturing shoelaces, you could begin a model by entering your start-up, design and tooling costs into your electronic spreadsheet software. Your formulas would use these items as fixed costs included in the total "cost of sales," along with rental on factory space, salaries of manufacturing workers, utilities and all the rest.

But your formulas would use the costs of raw materials—plastic for the shoelace nibs and cotton for the shoelace itself—as variable costs. Using separate formulas for each raw material—formulas that refer to cells containing cost figures and to other cells containing sales volume data— the computer would automatically calculate the cost of raw materials in total, and also per unit manufactured and sold.

On the revenue side of your model, you could specify an average sale price per shoelace. Or you could make the model more elaborate—and possibly more accurate (if you set up the formulas correctly)—by specifying the quantities you sell (or expect to sell) at each price point. The software would then be able to compute the total revenues, the total costs, and display the bottom-line difference. Because you've built a model whose formulas use cell references rather than fixed numbers, you can easily change the value in the cells containing the various volume, unit cost and revenue figures, instantly causing the model to recompute the formulas and display the latest results.

Another advantage of the electronic spreadsheet is that you can easily make changes and additions to previous work, and build on a basic model by adding more complexity and detail. For example, you might change the monthly utilities charges in your model from a fixed number reflecting monthly averages to a formula based on the actual cost of electricity and water and the number of hours the manufacturing equipment will be run (a number that could be based on a formula incorporating the same volume of sales you used in computing the cost of materials). With this arrangement, when you change the value for sales volume, the spreadsheet software changes not only the costs of raw materials but also the utility charges. You might further expand the model by factoring in collections, writing a formula that adds any carrying charges to total revenues and subtracts any uncollectible debts. You could also modify the model to calculate (and include the bottom-line impact of) commissions for sales people.

In practice, there are only two limits on the changes and additions you can make to your computer models. The technical limit is the (relatively huge) capacity of the electronic software to hold all the numbers and formulas you want to enter. The more important limit is your ability and available time to express business operations accurately in numbers and formulas.

"What If" Analysis

You've probably noted that electronic spreadsheets make it very easy to change the values in particular cells. This is the basis of the software's powerful capability to display the effects a change will have on the results produced by your mathematical model. "What if" analysis is simply the consideration of differing results produced by changes to the values of a mathematical model. It's named for the basic type of question you'll be asking as you proceed: "What if we change the price we charge? What if we sell twice as many items?" and so forth. (Most times, you change the input values—that is, those on which the software bases its calculations. For example: "If we sell 10,000 units, how much will we make?" But other times, you'll want to experiment to see exactly what input values produce a specific result. For example: "How many units must we sell to make $100,000?" Some electronic spreadsheet software will calculate formulas in reverse, selecting input values to generate the results you have specified. But you can accomplish this manually with any electronic spreadsheet software.)

The fundamental assumption of "what if" analysis is that your model is accurate. To be sure about this, build your model in stages or phases, and test it frequently with a simple series of input values, so you can quickly check for accuracy. For example, if you double the number of unit sales and the resulting profit doesn't double, there's probably something wrong with your model. (There are whole books and seminars on this subject.) Once you're convinced your computer model accurately reflects the business operation—or the plan for a new business operation—you're analyzing, you can begin with "what if" analysis.

Let's assume you start by varying the most important input values. For example, in the manufacturing model we discussed in the previous section, you would almost always want to investigate first the impact of changes to sales volume, raw materials costs, and sales price. By systematically changing these numbers, the spreadsheet software shows you how to optimize the factors you can control.

Afterward, you can "fine-tune" your analysis by checking the impact of secondary factors, such as costs, lead times, overhead, and so forth. If you want to rethink your analysis and assumptions, and perhaps modify the model's values and formulas to more accurately reflect the real-world business operation you're attempting to model, you can easily do so.

One thing that computer and software cannot do, however, is protect you from the most common mental trap of electronic spreadsheets and "what if" analysis: the unspoken belief that whatever you create within the spreadsheet will automatically happen in the real world. Many people build a complex model, optimize it carefully, then work with "what if" analysis until they get everything just the way they want it. But they fail to make a success of the project because they blur the line between their mathematical model and reality. Never forget that a computer model—no matter how comprehensive or accurate—only reflects reality as you understand it. Fiddling with sales figures on the model has nothing whatever to do with changing sales figures in the real world. If you can't or don't do the work to make your ideas and assumptions a reality, even the finest electronic model won't be worth the paper it's printed on.

Spreadsheet Accounting
Because the electronic spreadsheet is so easy to set up with column totals and labels, it's a natural tool for simplified business accounting. As I've mentioned, there is special-purpose software designed for business accounting. But you can do many of the same tasks with general-purpose spreadsheet software. In most cases, you'll want to start simply, and build more and more features into your accounting spreadsheet as you go.

If you want your spreadsheet to do more elaborate accounting, you may find one or more "sample" data files that provide the basis for sophisticated electronic accounting. Other spreadsheet packages are supported by software called "add in" modules, which actually change how the electronic spreadsheet appears and operates. Some of the most popular "add in" modules change a simple spreadsheet to a sophisticated accounting application.

Spreadsheet Databases
Innovated by Lotus Development Corporation, spreadsheet database capabilities are much appreciated by some users, disdained by others. Whether or not they have value for you is something no one else can decide.

Spreadsheet databases operate on the same record and field arrangement used in the best database management software. Within the spreadsheet, each row is a record, each column is a field. You enter the information as you would in any spreadsheet, but by maintaining uniform record and field structure, you allow the computer to search, select and sort the information.

Spreadsheet databases are most useful when you want to perform both spreadsheet computations and database operations on the same set of data. However, when you have a great deal of data and overworked hardware, database operations can be considerably slower within the spreadsheet than they would be within a specialized database management package.

Electronic Spreadsheet Automatic Functions
The automatic functions built into electronic spreadsheet software are intended to simplify the process of writing formulas and building models. Each automatic function is simply a mathematical formula that has been programmed into the spreadsheet software. You can quickly and easily insert one or more of these functions into a cell or a formula. If the one you want is not available, you can always refer to a book of formulas and manually enter it.

Spreadsheet automatic functions can generally be divided into the following categories: statistical, string, database, logical, mathematical, financial, and date and time. Statistical functions include averages, means, medians, standard deviation and variance. String functions—not available in all spreadsheet software—allow text to be used as numbers or convert numbers to text for special-purpose computations. Database functions allow the software to search, sort and select rows of data that meet certain criteria you specify. Logical functions test the values in specified cells to see if they do or do not meet certain conditions, and thus allow sophisticated computations to be controlled on the basis of other computations. Mathematical functions include random number generation, trigonometry, square roots, logs, and exponents. Addition, subtraction, division and multiplication are handled within formulas simply by entering the appropriate sign. Financial functions include a broad range of formulas for computing payments and values, rates of return and depreciation. Date and time functions allow the spreadsheet to perform calendar and clock arithmetic, to facilitate computations like the amount of interest due after a certain number of days, or the hourly rate earned during a single-payment project.

Different electronic spreadsheet packages will contain differing combinations of these functions. Since most of the functions automate standard (if advanced) mathematical concepts, and since there are a hundred or more such functions commonly available, it's not appropriate to discuss them in detail in this book. However, the presence or absence of particular functions in an electronic spreadsheet package you are evaluating can help you choose between otherwise equal packages.

Spreadsheet Formatting and Printing
Since their introduction and rapid acceptance during the early 1980s, the only major improvement in electronic spreadsheet software has been better formatting of printed output. The first spreadsheets printed like typewriters, and could output only what you saw on the screen. The newer ones can print the underlying formulas as easily as the calculated values normally displayed. They also offer a variety of typefaces and sizes, borders, page headers and footers, column and row labels, and more. Some can print sideways (with rows printed along the length of the page instead of the width) on command. Those intended for use with a graphical user interface tend to have nearly as much formatting capability as a word processor!

These formatting capabilities may be important if you plan to print spreadsheet materials directly from the spreadsheet software. But if you plan to export data into other applications—like a word processor or a database manager—the electronic spreadsheet's formatting capabilities will prove less important to you.

Graphing Data in Electronic Spreadsheets
In recent years, there has been a trend among software developers to include graphing capabilities in electronic spreadsheet packages. (The details of computerized graphing capabilities are covered under "The Graphs and Presentation Programs," on p. 90) One advantage of this approach is that you get two software capabilities in one—presumably for one price, as well. That is, you can use the software not only to perform spreadsheet computations, but simply to record numerical information and print it in graphic form. Another advantage of combined spreadsheet and graphics capabilities is that data entered into your spreadsheet for computations are immediately available for graphing. If you had separate spreadsheet and graphing software packages, you would somehow have to transfer the data from the spreadsheet to the graphic application before you could graph it.

Exporting Data From Electronic Spreadsheets
As you probably recognize, it's comforting to know your investment in data is protected by a good export capability in each of the software packages you use most frequently, allowing you to transfer your precious data for use in other applications or for use in a more powerful software package that replaces the one you've been using.

At a minimum, software should be able to export information into a simple ASCII data file. Once this is done, you can use word processing or text editing software to manipulate the data into whatever organization or arrangement the receiving software requires. However, you can avoid these data manipulations if the exporting software and the importing software are capable of using the same data file format. This is not as haphazard as you may think, because software developers tend to use half a dozen or more file formats as "de facto" standards for data transfer.

As graphical user interfaces and multitasking operating systems gain in popularity, more and more software reaching the market conforms to an accepted data interchange standard. Offering this kind of shared capability for data exchange may not count as a crucial factor in selecting software, but it's a great timesaver if available when needed.

The Word Processor
First generation word processors were simple text editors, designed to allow programmers to write and edit computer instructions on the display screen, generally one line at a time in some computer programming language. In my view, even this rudimentary word processing software was a remarkable breakthrough because it provided a totally new capability to review written material and meticulously change the tiny details that distinguish powerful, persuasive prose from ordinary writing.

Over the years, word processing software has been extremely well received by many people who are not computer programmers, and today it is virtually standard software for about 85 percent of computers used in business. One reason for this broad acceptance is that word processing software provides so many opportunities to save time and improve writing. Another is that later generations of word processing software have steadily offered faster, easier, and better formatting and printing capabilities, which nearly always results in better *looking* documents, even if the words don't make any more sense than they did before.

The latest word processors offer important business advantages and productivity improvements no typewriter ever imagined. In fact, without giving up any of the low-end capabilities, word processors are steadily adding built-in graphics and rapidly catching up to desktop publishing software, which I discuss elsewhere in this book. For now, though, let's consider the central features you should examine when selecting a computerized word processing software package.

The most fundamental advantage of word processing over handwritten or typewritten work is the ability to do endless editing and still print a clean copy of the draft material at any time. You can reword your ideas, switch around sentences or paragraphs and add or delete information to your heart's content. While typewritten or handwritten pages would quickly become messy and perhaps illegible, your word processing document is always fresh, clean and clear. Word processing is a significant timesaver, if only because you don't have to retype the whole document every time you make a change.

Because this is the fundamental use of word processing software, pay special attention to the keystroke sequences required for basic text editing: enter, overtype, delete, copy, move, and so forth. Competing software packages do this bedrock word processing work in vastly different ways. Some have very intuitive command structures, some don't. Some use graphical interfaces, some don't. There's no absolute basis for judging which is "better," but there's every likelihood you'll personally prefer one software system more than another.

A second feature of word processing software is the ability to make "global changes." Thus, if you spell a name wrong, you can correct every occurrence of the misspelling with a single command sequence. Similarly, if you have a file with extra punctuation or spaces, you can remove them or make other changes in thousands of locations automatically.

Modern word processing packages also format printed materials very nicely, which makes a better overall impression on everyone who sees your drafts and your finished materials. Because your text is automated, you can easily produce a new, clean copy with a simple computer command, too. Even when the printer is limited to fixed spacing and a single typeface and size, word processing software can make sure a document's tabs, indents, margins and other formatting elements are consistent and attractive. It can also make sure all documents have a consistent, high-quality appearance. When properly installed with a compatible letter-quality page printer, word processing software can give documents a "published" appearance by using proportional spacing and attractive type styles.

Some word processing software offers a WYSIWYG—or "what you see is what you get"—display. With this, you needn't imagine what formatting codes may do to your document, nor must you print the document several times, making adjustments until you obtain the final appearance you want. With WYSIWYG, you simply make adjustments until the screen looks right, knowing the printed page will automatically look the same. However, for complex technical reasons some WYSIWYG capabilities are imperfect. That is, on particular computer systems a document's screen appearance and printed appearance won't correspond exactly. If WYSIWYG is important to you, make sure to test the software on the hardware you'll be using to see how well they work together.

Once a document is completed, printed and delivered, you're normally done with it. But with word processing software, you automatically have the ability to reuse your previous documents over and over. Often called "boilerplate," such material helps you obtain advantages from your word processing software you can't get from a typewriter. For example, once you compose a sales letter, you can use it as boilerplate again and again, each time with appropriate changes for the present situation. After you negotiate a sales contract with one customer, it can become boilerplate for beginning negotiations with the next.

To facilitate use of boilerplate, though, word processing software should make it very easy to hold one document open while you review a second document. You should also find it easy to import some or all of the second document into the first one. If you must import all of the second document, using boilerplate is much easier when the software offers convenient ways to delete large blocks of any excess material you've imported.

Mail merge is a powerful capability you get with a great many word processing packages. Essentially, mail merge is an automated form of boilerplate that allows you to create an original document, and then print one copy of it for each person on your mailing list. In addition to inserting the appropriate names and addresses, mail merge can also include other information: the expiration date of an insurance policy, the details of the customer's last order from you, or anything else you can include in a properly arranged data file. Because mail merge is such a powerful capability, some users find it very complex to set up correctly. A single comma misplaced in your data file can throw off the insertion of data for a thousand printed pages that follow. A mistake in your original document will be repeated in every copy. In evaluating word processing software for its mail merge capabilities, try to ascertain how well you understand the commands for using it. To find out if the directions are clear and concise, you might want to try setting up a practice mail merge, just to see if you can do it.

Another important factor to weigh in your selection of word processing software is its flexibility for doing mail merge with data files from other programs. Some software vendors assert their products can do mail merge reliably with ASCII data files. But when you try, you find the software doesn't perform as advertised and you're forced to set up your data files in the word processing program's own (perhaps difficult to follow) format. Other technical matters may also interfere with proper functions.

Aside from mail merge, other features you'll want to evaluate within word processing software include on-line spell-checking, thesaurus and grammatical analysis. Spell-checking capabilities are quite common, but some systems are considerably more convenient and powerful than others. For example, a package may not let you spell-check only a portion of the document, or cancel the spell-checking in the middle of the document. There's also the question of secondary dictionaries. If you work with specialized, technical words, you'll want to be able to add them to the spell-checking software's dictionary. If you use several sets of specialized words, you'll prefer a software package that lets you select which secondary dictionary file to use.

Graphical and menu-oriented interfaces often produce big differences in how easily you can learn to use a particular word processing package, and how much you enjoy it when you do. You may need years to master all the features of an advanced word processor but a simplified user interface may make it practical for writing even the shortest notes, and allow most people to begin doing meaningful work with only a few minutes of training. Again, there's no one best user interface. Simply experiment with different packages and make your own decision regarding which one you prefer.

One major difference between word processing software packages is the ability to incorporate text, graphics and sound into a document. If the software can handle this, dry reports and memos can be dressed up with charts, graphs, logos, and other emphatics. In some cases, the word processing software can create and print its own graphics and emphatics, as well as manipulate those created with other software.

Multicolumn capabilities also vary greatly from one word processing package to another. When you can lay out more than one column on a page, it's easy to prepare newsletters and other materials to be printed with the shorter line lengths many people consider more attractive and easier to read. Adding extra columns also lets you prepare tables and other visual presentations of data. When your printouts will use today's attractive "proportional" type fonts, test the software to make sure it neatly aligns every line in every column.

One of the most useful features available in some of today's word processing packages is the "automatic outlining" capability. This harnesses the power of the computer to help organize, reorganize, and present information—anything from a business plan to a daily memo—far more quickly and easily than you can without it. Automatic outlining makes it easy to insert, delete and move outline elements. When you make a change, the software automatically relabels the entire outline— using any of several styles. This capability may also let you compress or expand any portion of the outline, so you can more easily ignore all the text but the portion on which you're concentrating.

The Forecasting Program

Many organizations are not set up for forecasting, and are content to do without it. But larger organizations, and those that want to plan for the future, often spend considerable resources in noting past performance and projecting future potential. Sales projections, budget projections, needed inventory levels, and future price levels are only a few of the subjects that yield to forecasting methods. Naturally, the right computer software makes forecasting far easier and more accurate than forecasts developed manually.

When evaluating forecasting software, consider first the problem of input. Accurate forecasting depends not only on following the right procedures, but on starting with the correct data. In most cases, using larger quantities of relevant data will result in more accurate projections. So a legitimate concern is where the data to be analyzed will come from, and how it will be made available to the forecasting software. Because the need to input large quantities of data is so critical in forecasting, you'll want to investigate the software's power to read various data file formats. Pay particular attention to its compatibility with the formats available from any software packages—such as databases or accounting programs—that already contain data you'll want to analyze.

Another concern is data output. Once the analysis and forecasting are complete, you'll want to make some use of this information. You may want to print it as a self-contained report, or you may want to include it in other documents. You may want to create good-looking charts and graphs, or you may want to use the forecast data as the basis for an entire presentation—on slides or with computerized animation. None of this is possible, however, unless the forecasting software makes it so. To print the data, the software must communicate with an available printer and be programmed to make use of its capabilities. To include forecast material in other documents, or to use it within charting, graphing or presentation programs, the forecasting package must be able to convert its information to a standard ASCII file or some other compatible data file format. The issue of compatibility is also important in a more general sense. Obviously, the forecasting software must be compatible with the computer on which you want it to run. But if you have an unusual printer or display screen, or if you have a network, the software may be incompatible with any or all of these.

Assuming the software will operate as you need and want it to within your existing computer system(s), you can begin to evaluate how well it does its basic job of forecasting the future. Some software offers a single forecasting technique, and in fact may not even indicate what that is. You simply feed in numbers and read off the result, without ever knowing what calculations or assumptions the software has made on your data.

More sophisticated forecasting software will offer a variety of forecasting techniques—such as absolute change, percentage change, and regression analysis—and give you a chance not only to choose which one to employ, but to compare the results of the various methodologies on a single set of historical data. Software that can be set to make forecasts based on a portion of the available historical data can be very reassuring, because you can try making forecasts by means of various methodologies on the first part of the data and see which ones come closest to the actual historical record shown in the second part. Once you know which forecasting methodology most accurately projected the recent past on the basis of the more distant past, you can feel confident that similarly calculated projections about the future will be relatively reliable, too.

The Graphics and Presentation Programs
Graphics is an area of tremendous interest and excitement among computer users. Today's faster processors, larger computer memories, and more detailed, color-capable display screens have made graphics a central facet of computer use. Aside from their use in a "graphical user interface," computer graphics capabilities are rapidly gaining acceptance in the basic portfolio of business application software, right beside word processing, electronic spreadsheets, accounting and database management software. If you don't use some form of computer graphics presently, you probably will sometime soon. Computer graphics can be used to:

• Improve the appearance of printed reports and other presentations.
• Convert difficult and obscure lists of numbers into vivid graphics.
• Add visual appeal to talks and speeches.
• Give visual clarification to difficult ideas and complex relationships.
• Decrease the cost and shorten the lead-time requirements of designing and using graphics in brochures, booklets, catalog pages and other printed materials.

Image-Oriented Graphics Software
Image-oriented graphics software includes several different types of programs. Some allow you to use the cursor—which functions as a pen, brush, spray can or a variety of other marking tools—to "paint" or "draw" on the computer screen anything that you can imagine. Later, you can use a wide variety of other tools and commands to edit and modify the images you've created. Other image-oriented graphics programs are based on a programming language rather than drawing tools. You describe images in detail, and the software presents them on the computer screen. If you rewrite the description, the image changes accordingly. These programs can be used to produce signs, logos and logotypes, to retouch images and create or manipulate other visual materials.

A few image-oriented programs are set up to present drawings of three-dimensional objects, using either "wire frame" techniques or shading and lighting to present believable "solid" objects. Some 3D programs allow the viewer's point of view to be moved anywhere around or inside the computer images. These programs can be used for a variety of architectural, engineering, construction, design and decoration-related work. They can also be used to create images for use in printed or other visual materials. Still other programs, generally intended for more scientific or experimental applications, start with a basic description or image and operate on it automatically to create abstract images of startling beauty and complexity.

Images can be drawn or described within this type of graphics software. Or they can be captured usually by means of a scanner. Some graphics software allows you to "clip" any part of any screen display that appears on your computer, and subsequently use it as an image to be modified or printed like any other. There is even an electronic form of "clip art"—simplified standard drawings you can purchase at relatively low prices and use in your own work without licensing or royalty worries. Thousands of pieces of clip art are actively marketed and widely used in computerized imaging software.

Once a computerized image has been created, captured or clipped, the software generally allows you to make all manner of changes to it, as well as to how you see it. Graphics software may employ such familiar noncomputerized editing techniques as changing the point of view, cropping, and changing image brightness or color. It may allow the image to be zoomed, moved, tipped, rotated or flipped about one or more axes. Some of the software designed to show 3D images will also allow the image to be seen in two dimensions to improve the viewer's clarity and understanding of the shapes being displayed.

Because the image is computerized, the right software will allow it to be electronically reversed (black for white, or vice versa), skewed, scaled up or down, sharpened or softened. If the image is too large to be seen on the screen all at once, the displayed area can be scrolled or panned to reveal other parts of the image. Both colors and shades of grey can be blended to form gradations of density, hues, shades and tints. Some software supports "layers" within an image, which works as though various graphic elements were drawn on separate transparencies meant to be stacked up and shown all together. This allows different parts of the image to be faded, sized, moved and otherwise manipulated separately.

Technically, a computer image contains hundreds of thousands or even millions of picture elements, or "pixels"—like the painting technique of pointillism. Some software allows the user to edit each pixel individually. Although editing at this level can require a great deal of time, it allows highly detailed control over the final image.

Another technical factor is how the software stores the image electronically. If it records each pixel individually in computer memory or disk storage, the image is said to be "bitmapped," literally a collection of pixels. However, some software stores each part of an image simply as the directions needed to draw it. This technique is called "vector" graphics. Vector graphics work better than bitmapped graphics when images are going to be scaled up to larger sizes, because enlarging bitmapped graphics tends to result in jagged curves rather than smooth ones. Also vector graphic files tend to be much smaller than bitmapped graphic files for comparable images.

There are many different data file formats used with graphics. Graphics files usually end with such suffixes as: PCX, DFX, TIF, IFF, LBM, TGA, ICO, CLP, RLE, WPG, DIB, JAS, MSP, RAS, GIF, MAC, BMP, IMG, or others—each one identifying a specific file format and graphics type. You probably shouldn't be overly concerned about this, except to be sure that any software you acquire can make use of any graphics files you are likely to use with it.

Another significant difference from one graphics software package to another concerns whether they handle graphic elements as "objects." Given a particular graphics image, it can be stored electronically as a single, unitary image covering the entire screen area, or it can be made up of a series of separate "objects." The difference is profound in terms of your ability to modify what you see. If you draw two overlapping circles using an ordinary "paint" program, for example, you cannot separate them afterward. But if you draw the same circles using "object" oriented graphics software, each circle remains independent of the other, allowing you to move, size, skew and separately edit each one to your heart's content.

Other computer editing functions that can be applied to images include: copy, cut and paste (for whole images as well as objects and/or clipped portions of the image), undo (which returns the image to what it was before you made the last change), add or remove shadows, and automatically draw standard shapes (including, circles, ellipses, square and rounded boxes, and sometimes even polygons). Some software will automatically eliminate the lines that should be "hidden" behind solid shapes within the image. Some offer automatic "curve fitting," allowing you to specify a few points and have the software automatically draw a smoothly curved line between them.

Many drawing programs allow you to change the pen/line width, add arrowheads and tails at the ends of lines, paint with an airbrush, fill an image space a choice of patterns or colors, and add text to the image (either typed or electronically read from a file). Some software will automatically lay text along a curved line in the image. A few offer an on-screen grid, continual displays of the cursor's X-Y coordinates, and precise measuring tools to help align graphic elements where you want them. With many packages, you can surround a graphic object with tiny handles, which you can then "pull" with the cursor to bend and modify the object in a predictable manner. One rather sophisticated graphics software function is to "trace" a bitmapped image (brought into the computer through a scanner or generated electronically), and convert it to the vector graphics format. This permits the traced image to be modified more accurately and easily.

In evaluating software for possible acquisition, concentrate on the tasks you want it to perform, and test to make sure it has the functions and features to do the required work quickly and easily. Also, make sure the package is compatible (insofar as necessary) with other software you will be using in your business operations.

Business Graphics Software

Using many of the same capabilities and functions described for image-oriented graphics software, business graphics software aims to computerize the process of preparing and printing displays of both text material and numerical charts and tables. Most business graphics software assumes you understand the data and know how you want to display it. The software merely simplifies the process of displaying raw numbers or complex ideas as vivid, exciting graphics.

For text-oriented material, business graphics software can produce attractive printed signs or screens on the computer display. Some software also allows the "screens" to be quickly and inexpensively converted into photographic slides or overhead transparencies you can project on a large screen for viewing by hundreds of people. These screens, or slides, can contain quotations, titles and supporting items, clip art, logos or other graphic images. The better programs offer detailed control over typefaces, type sizes, object placement, color, borders, the shapes of "bullets" used to set off supporting items (normally little dots, graphic elements used as bullets can be anything from tiny telephones to graceful arrowheads), and more.

Numerically oriented business graphics tend to be pie charts, bar charts, X-Y graphs and scatter graphs. These lines, circles, dots and other graphic elements are meant to represent and quickly show the relationships between numerical values that would otherwise have to be printed, read and laboriously compared. Business graphics also includes a wide range of more sophisticated charts that have evolved from these basic forms: stacked line and bar charts, exploded pie charts, area graphs and histograms, each of which can display single or multiple sets of data simultaneously.

Business graphics software is generally capable of creating a chart based on data you either enter manually or have the computer "read" electronically from an existing computer data file. Although useful charts can present just a few numbers that are easy to enter by hand, many business situations require charts to display dozens or hundreds of precise, up-to-the-minute figures. Some charts must be redrawn every week, month or quarter using the latest data. That's why the ability to make charts from data already gathered and processed in other software is a major advantage for business graphics software. Before you acquire any business graphics package, make sure you know its capabilities with regard to reading electronic data files produced from your other business software.

Some software makes it easy to save a completed chart to disk, and then to regenerate it at a later time using more recent data. Other software tightly integrates the data with the chart specifications, and thus makes it more difficult to generate a chart updated with new data. Each package has its own way of labeling the data. Often, the software provides one or more spaces for labeling the chart as a whole, each axis, and each data set on the graph. The chart can become crowded very quickly, particularly when "simplified" software doesn't leave you much control over label placement or size. Make sure the software you're considering allows enough room and flexibility to legibly label the charts you'll want to create.

One mixed blessing is the feature called automatic scaling. If you're entering a chart with data from .01 to 1,000, for example, software with this feature will be smart enough to draw a chart with enough room for all the values it will be plotting. However, this feature can outsmart you when you're trying to make a consistent set of graphs showing vastly different sets of data. The computer may want them to have different scales, making chart-to-chart comparisons misleading. It's desirable to have a manual override for the auto-scaling feature.

Presentation Software

Closely related to business graphics software, presentation software provides a whole new set of chart presentation capabilities. You can use presentation software to add visual punch or support to a sales speech, demonstrate a project, or drive home a point. On-screen presentations can also help with training. Any information that can be presented in print can be presented—often less expensively and more effectively— with computer presentation software. Some presentation software incorporates the same portfolio of chart creation capabilities as business graphics software (discussed in the previous section), but other packages require that the graphics already exist.

Regardless of how you develop a series of graphic screens, presentation software gives you excellent control over when and how they can be displayed on the computer screen. (If you choose to have the screens converted to slides or overhead graphics, you move them out of the arena of presentation software and beyond the scope of this book. It requires highly specialized software for the computer to operate the projection machinery used to present the screens in these new formats.)

With presentation software, a simple series of slides that each list three or four points can be presented more interestingly as, for example, an animated list. The software can reveal each point on the first slide one at a time, then dissolve to a second slide and similarly reveal its points one at a time. If a graphics screen incorporates a set of objects, presentation software can move one object in relation to the others, allowing the sun to rise or a ball to bounce. By changing rapidly from one screen to a subtly different screen, presentation software can make it appear that a bomb explodes or a sad face changes to a happy one. Presentation software packages allow you to establish any of a wide variety of fades, dissolves, wipes, and other transitions from one graphics screen to another. You can control these manually in real time, or create a script.

A script is a series of code words and timing factors that you enter in a "behind the scenes" part of the presentation software. You save the script to disk and retrieve it again for later use or for modification. Once you activate the script, the presentation software puts on the show you have scripted either under automatic or semi-automatic control. If you select automatic control, the show proceeds without you. If you select semi-automatic control, the software executes the next step in your script only when you press a key or click the mouse.

If the presentation software has an "endless loop" feature, it converts the computer to a sales presentation device. The computer can stand alone on a counter or in a store window and execute a script showing a sales message—or any other show you've created—over and over again without taking a lunch break or getting tired.

Chart Software

The most common types of charts in this category are organization (org) charts and flow charts. These are basically a set of symbols—squares, rounded boxes, circles, triangles, diamonds and so forth—labeled with people's names and titles or with checkpoints or processes, which are arranged on paper and connected by lines to visually demonstrate their relationship to one another.

These are useful not only for showing how people are supposed to report to one another, and who has responsibility for what within an organization, but to clarify relationships between people, processes and things that might take a thousand words to describe. A good org chart helps everyone understand how an organization is supposed to operate. A good flow chart makes clear how the various parts and processes of a product, project or business fit together, and the relative importance of each one.

Generally, the difficult part of creating an org or flow chart is getting all the labels correct and specifying the various relationships between them. Drawing the chart manually to reflect that information is merely tedious and time-consuming. And that's precisely why it doesn't get done as often as it probably should, and why computerizing org and flow charts can create major improvements in efficiency and productivity.

Once the chart information is entered into the computer, it's very easy to make changes, and takes only a few keystrokes to generate a new and completely up-to-date version of the chart.

Some chart software is based on an outline or other arrangement of text that will constitute the labels on the finished chart. By moving these labels around or otherwise adjusting their relationships, you provide the software with information on the relative positions the labels should have when the chart is drawn. Because there can be many subtleties or ambiguities in an org or flow chart, some charting software provides a means to control precisely where to locate each symbol on the finished chart.

Once all the details are entered, the computer quickly draws the symbols and their labels, and lays out the connecting lines to complete the org or flow chart. When a relationship or label must be changed, you do it on the underlying information, and the computer quickly redraws the chart to reflect the new situation.

The Keyboard Macro Manager

As you gain familiarity with using a computer to accomplish more work in less time, you'll grow increasingly appreciative of a utility program (or software capability) known as the "macro" manager. Properly set up, macros can greatly speed your work with a computer, or can make it easy for someone with little or no computer training to operate complex software, generate detailed reports, compile and process intricate financial data, or otherwise use a computer for sophisticated business purposes.

As I briefly noted under "Database Manager Programming Languages and Macros" above, a macro is a computer capability to store and reuse a sequence of keystrokes, mouse movements or other computer inputs. For simplicity, I'll be discussing keyboard macros, but the macro concepts can be applied to other computer actions, as well.

Basically, a macro simplifies the process of operating your computer. For example, if it takes fifteen keystrokes to cause a database program to print a specific report, you can "record" those fifteen keystrokes as a macro then "play back" the macro by pressing only one or two keys. Instantly, the macro capability takes control of the computer and repeats the original fifteen keystrokes just as if you were entering them at the keyboard. Effectively, the macro now allows the computer to perform automatically a process it would otherwise perform only manually.

The simplest use of a macro is to repeat a difficult keystroke sequence, say a long and complicated customer name, without the possibility of introducing a new typographical error each time you enter it. Once you correctly record the name as a macro, it will always be entered correctly, and you need never type it manually again.

You'll also find macro capabilities useful to record the keystrokes needed for complex computer operations—generating reports, processing transactions, modifying or reformatting large data files, or anything else of a repetitive nature. The macro not only records and reissues the keystroke commands correctly, it allows you to do something else while the computer processes on its own.

There is a danger, however. If you build a macro to modify a data file and the data file is not consistently structured, or somehow the macro gets out of synchronization with the file, you could inadvertently make changes to data where you didn't want them. You could even erase data. Like "the sorcerer's apprentice," a macro doesn't know why or where it is supposed to operate, rather it mindlessly executes a sequence of computer commands. It's up to you to make sure your macro does exactly what you intend it to do, and nothing else.

Normally, each macro is stored with its own triggering keystroke or keystroke combination—usually including the "Alternate" key or "Control" key so the macro doesn't preclude normal typing or application software commands. For example, you may record the sequence "Constantinople" to be triggered by the keystroke combination "Alternate-C". You can type "C" as often as you like; the computer types "Constantinople" under macro control only when you hold down the "Alternate" key *and* press the "C" key.

With most application software, there are plenty of "Alternate" or "Control" keystroke combinations available for macros. But some application packages use so many keystroke combinations there are relatively few combinations left open for macros. To solve this problem, more advanced macro capabilities support on-screen menus. This way, one reserved keystroke combination can open a menu offering literally dozens of prerecorded macros (including perhaps some additional submenus). Macro menus are very easy to work with because you do not have to memorize special keystroke combinations. You simply pick a choice from among the possibilities presented on the display screen, and the computer then goes through its paces automatically.

Notice that we've been talking in terms of "macro capabilities." This term is intended to refer to either the macro capabilities built into some application software, or macro utility software specifically designed to add macro capabilities to any application software. Macro utility software may support macro menus, ordinary macro keystroke combinations or both. If the macro utility software permits loading files of stored macros, you can set up many different macro control systems—each containing instructions for a different set of keyboard macros—and use them to control many different application programs. Macro capabilities built into a software application obviously can't be used for controlling other applications. From the point of view of the user, however, how the macro capabilities are delivered may not matter, so long as they are available to help control a difficult or complex application.

Whether you're evaluating macro utility software or the macro capabilities built into a specific application, here are the most important macro features you should test:

Macro Recording Capability

Most often, you record a macro by entering a reserved keystroke combination that tells the macro capability to start recording subsequent keystrokes. From then on, everything you type is recorded for later playback. When you've completed all the computer functions you want to include in your macro, you press the same or another reserved keystroke combination to stop recording. The macro capability also prompts you for the keystroke or keystroke-combination you want as the trigger for these recorded keystrokes. This method—often called "learn mode" or "keystroke capture"—is the easiest for most macros you'll want to record, because it requires the fewest extra keystrokes. It also requires little planning or advance thinking. You can record the macros you want as you work with the computer on any of your usual tasks.

But a different recording method works better in other situations. "Keystroke recall" is a capability for recording a macro by browsing through your most recent fifty, one hundred, or more keystrokes and clipping the ones you'd like to include in a macro. This technique is useful when you don't know in advance that you'd like to record the next series of keystrokes. For example, you may enter the keystrokes to generate a database report, then realize you'll want to repeat that report every week. Once you discover that you want certain keystrokes in a macro, "keystroke recall" lets you put them there without having to repeat your previous work.

A related macro recording capability is "browse and clip." This method lets you select characters from any display screen and save them as a macro for later playback. You'll find this approach most useful when you're browsing through data files and realize you want to re-enter in another location some of the information you're presently viewing.

Macro Editing Capability

Whether you're recording or clipping keystrokes for macros, sooner or later you're going to include a keystroke that's wrong for the macro you're trying to build. This is when macro editing becomes important.

The information to be played back in a macro is normally held in computer memory or on disk. Either way, the macro capability should make it easy to view and edit these keystrokes. Some macro capabilities provide their own editing features, others create macro files that any word processor can edit. In general, you can nearly always edit macro files on disk. Your most important concern is to determine how quickly and easily you can repair a mistake or make a change to a macro. How long does it take to get into the "edit mode" and start working with the macro data file? Must you retype the whole macro, or can you retype just the part you want to change? Can an existing macro be copied and then modified into a separate, different macro? When editing a macro, how easily can you test the modified version in action?

Macro Save and Retrieve

Since the information played back in a macro is generally stored in a file, it's important to evaluate how quickly and easily you can save a new macro to a file and/or retrieve an existing macro file so you can make use of it.

While you're considering the macro's data files, determine the maximum length of a single macro (that is, the maximum number of keystrokes that can be played back automatically without user intervention) and the maximum number of macros that can be ready for use at one time. Since macros ready for immediate use are generally held in computer memory rather than on disk, this aspect of a macro capability usually depends on the computer's overall use of its memory. Without getting involved in bits and bytes, just make sure the macro capability you're acquiring works with your computer system and with any application you want it to control.

Macro Playback or Execution

All you really need to know about macro playback or execution is that the macro capability you're planning to acquire can do the job you want. But there are some technical considerations you may want to investigate.

Can one macro call another? In advanced uses of macro capabilities, this is a valuable parlor trick. For example, you may record the word *Christmas* on key F7, and the word *Merry* on key F6. Then you may record keys F6 and F7 on "Alternate-C." If one macro can call another, then pressing "Alternate-C" will display *Merry Christmas*. But if one macro cannot call another, then pressing "Alternate-C" will trigger nothing, or whatever normal functions are associated with F6 and F7.

Can macro execution be interrupted? With some macro capabilities, triggering a macro relinquishes complete control over the computer. If a macro gets caught in a loop or starts destroying data, you can't easily stop it. Safer macro software contains a "macro break" command that lets you interrupt macro playback at any time.

Can multiple playback be commanded? For example, you may build a macro to find and delete the word *very*. If the macro capability supports multiple playback, you can have the software delete the next five or the next twenty instances of *very*. This is more convenient than triggering the macro five or twenty times.

Macro Loops

A different approach to multiple playback is to create a macro "loop." This is a series of keystroke commands that create an endless circle of instructions. For example, you could record a sequence of keystrokes that cause your word processing program to find the word *very*, delete it, and then restart the same macro again. Once you trigger this loop, it will continue to execute and thereby delete every instance of the word *very* (including the *very* within *everyone*) in the document.

Some macro capabilities will warn you that you've created an endless loop. Others refuse to record a macro containing an endless loop. Instead, you must record two or more macros that work together to create a loop. Some macro capabilities allow easy interruption of a loop. Others require you to hit the proper interrupt keys at just the right time or they won't work and the loop will continue. A few have a loop cancellation feature, in which an endless loop is automatically interrupted after ten or fifteen iterations.

Evaluate any macro capabilities you're considering to see if its endless loop features are compatible with how you intend to use the software.

Macro Menus

Macro menus are really nothing more than layers of macros made available in sequence. Triggering the first-layer macro displays a menu with other macros. Selecting one of these macros triggers computer commands or perhaps a menu displaying a third set of macros, and so forth.

Macro menus are attractive chiefly in two situations:

1) when people who don't have much training or savvy are going to be asked to perform fairly complicated computer operations, and

2) when you're trying to simplify and minimize highly repetitive computer operations for which you don't have enough keystroke combinations available.

Your ability to create, edit and use a macro menu depends on the menu capabilities the macro software contains. (It's rare to find menus in macro capabilities built into application software.) There is no right, wrong, good or bad features in this area. Simply evaluate the software to see how quickly and easily you can create, modify and work with macro menus.

Macro Windows

Macro windows are prompts your macro software displays during macro playback and/or menu selection to help the user understand what he or she should do. Macro windows can be very useful for people who don't know how to perform difficult or complex computer operations, or who do particular operations so infrequently that from one time to the next they forget how.

Macro windows can also be used to create a training system specifically for any piece of application software. It's time consuming, but possible to overlay some or all of the application's normal keystroke combinations with macros that display a window with relevant training information, and after a pause allow the selected command to execute normally.

Macro windows are a rather advanced capability that you need not consider unless you are looking to make use of them for a specific purpose.

Other Macro Functions

There are a great many other factors you can consider in evaluating and selecting macro software. Most of them are too technical to discuss here, but they are worth mentioning. If you feel they may be important to your decision, consult an expert who can help you include these factors in your evaluation.

- Memory usage refers to the quantity of computer memory absorbed by the macro capabilities. Obviously, the more memory given over to macros, the less is available for application software and data.
- Cut-and-paste refers to a capability (included with some macro utility software) to clip any portion of a display screen and enter it automatically into other software, or into a macro.
- The ability to temporarily disable the existing macros—either for one keystroke or until further notice—can be useful if the macro capability interferes with or blocks the issuing of important computer commands.
- Encryption is unrelated to macro capabilities, but is sometimes bundled with macro utility software, and can prove useful when you want to protect important information from potentially prying eyes.
- Text edit is also unrelated to macro capabilities, but is similarly bundled with some macro utility software. Text edit capabilities are useful with computers that cannot perform multi-tasking. The text edit capability of macro software allows you to start from one application and immediately look at, copy, delete, move, open and edit text files. When the text file work is complete, the software lets you return to your previous position within the main application.
- File management capabilities refer to the ability to copy, delete, rename or move files, as well as make and kill subdirectories, format

a disk, look inside a file and so forth. It can be very useful to do this from within a software application, wherever you obtain the capabilities from. If a macro utility offers file management capabilities, that's another item on the plus side of the ledger.

The Project Manager

Project management software incorporates elements of word processing, database management, flow charting, and in some cases accounting software. Although you can manage a project with the aid of these general-purpose software packages you may find a special-purpose package easier and more efficient to use because it offers precisely the project management features you want.

Project management software begins by recording lists of the people and the resources you have available to work on projects. It keeps track of each person's available hours, and in more sophisticated packages their strengths, skills, and experience, as well. Later, the software will help you decide how and when to assign these people to the many tasks that, when taken together, add up to project completion.

Resources include everything from available cash to equipment, tools, facilities, knowledge and everything else that will be applied in one way or another to completing a project. With project management software, you enter all this information into the computer, and then begin estimating the number of days needed to complete each task and the resources each one will require. Next, you specify target completion dates for the project, for its various chronological phases, and for individual tasks. The tasks generally fall into rough chronological order, but there are nuances. Some tasks must be done in sequence—for example, you cannot order building materials or start construction until you have first completed a building design—but other tasks can be done concurrently—for example, calculation of lease rates and preliminary marketing can easily take place during construction.

You also begin applying people and resources to each task—deciding, for example, that Sally will develop the initial design while Jerry will produce the marketing materials. As you make these decisions, the software helps you spot expectations of too many hours of work from any one person or too much utilization of any resource. Since one of the resources is money, project management software can help calculate the costs of particular tasks and phases, as well as a price tag for the entire project. The software can also help forecast how much money will be needed at major milestones during the project.

As the project proceeds, you use the software to record the inevitable changes in resource availability and personnel. Plans, as well as actual completion dates for each task can be updated automatically to reflect these changes. Most project management software can draw (on the display screen or on paper) a Gantt (bar) chart, a PERT (network) chart, and/or a critical-path chart for the entire project or any portion of it. Some can show discrepancies between planned and actual performance for completion dates, budgets, and resource usage. All this helps refine your plans and compensate for delays and other problems. The software can also show where bottlenecks are likely to occur—for example, when ten people will be trying to use the copier at the same time, or when one hundred tons of dirt will have to be moved with only one truck available to do the moving—far enough in advance for you to re-schedule to avert them or obtain more resources.

Because it includes a calendar—often one that takes into account work weeks, overtime constraints, planned vacations and holidays, time zone differences, and other factors—project management software can project the conclusion of a complex project with more accuracy that the average person. It can also print daily, weekly and monthly calendars and activity or assignment sheets for each person or team on the project.

Perhaps most importantly, the software can update its charts and calendars automatically to reflect even the smallest change in deadlines, personnel or resources. Thus, while project management software requires a great deal of input and constant updates during the course of the project, it normally pays for itself many times over by providing a better, clearer, more easily understood picture of the project plan, and of its status at any given moment. With this clearer understanding and simplified rescheduling and reallocating of resources, managing a project with a computer is far more efficient than doing it by hand.

The Statistics Program
Statistical analysis can be useful in many aspects of business operations, from manufacturing process control to market research. The right computer system makes short work of the computations necessary for summary, comparison, correlation, regression, nonparametric and other analyses. In addition, software can also help relatively untrained people

select the correct statistical analysis methods for a given set of data. Most of these "statistical consultant" packages operate by asking a series of questions about the data and your analytical focus. You answer, and the computer recommends a procedure for statistical analysis.

Once you have determined the best procedure to follow, software is available to perform the required analytical operations quickly and easily. Software functions can include sophisticated data management, and preprogrammed routines for any of the following:

- frequency distributions
- histograms
- calculation of the mean, median, mode, and standard deviations
- normality testing, and normal distributions
- combinations and permutations
- discrete probability distributions
- correlation analysis
- linear regression analysis
- time series analysis
- multiple comparisons

As you might expect, the practical use of these methods is beyond the scope of this book. But as always, I advise you to work with the software you are considering, to make sure it does what you want, the way you want before you acquire it.

4

......

Selecting Hardware

The natural inclination for novices who want to acquire a computer system is to look at hardware first, and software later. But this is a mistake. Hardware should be understood as simply the machinery that supports your software, which itself is merely intended to support your people, along with the business operations and procedures they hope to accomplish. Generally, letting hardware drive the computerization process is foolish and usually unsatisfying. It's far better to identify business operations and processes for computerization first, and select appropriate software on this basis. Once you know what software you'll be using, you can begin to make decisions regarding what types and capacities of hardware you require.

One difficulty many people encounter in choosing computer hardware is that there seems to be a steady improvement in computer capabilities, and a steady erosion of the price-performance curve. That is, a system priced at $3,000 last year may sell for $2,000 today. Most often, however, you can still spend $3,000 for a computer system, and it will provide far greater capabilities than last year's $3,000 system.

There is a natural urge to delay a computer acquisition for a week, a month, or longer in order to wait for the better system that is said to be almost ready for delivery. As you probably realize, this kind of reasoning will almost never let you make the purchase because there will always be another, better system on the horizon. In the meantime, you won't receive the benefits you would get from the presently available computer system. To avoid this kind of decision-making delay, people familiar with computers tend to think of them in the same category as automobiles. When you buy a car, you don't imagine it's the one and only car you'll ever acquire. You don't delay your purchase indefinitely because next year's model will have more power, better features or nicer styling. Instead, you simply acquire one that's presently available, and use it—for a year or a decade—until you feel ready to acquire another one. It's wise to do the same with computer hardware.

As an "escape hatch" from hardware roadblocks or dead ends in the future, always prefer equipment that meets widely accepted industry standards. Although standards change steadily, in most cases hardware that meets today's standards will be useful—even if in a diminished, peripheral role—for many years into the future. It's also a safe bet to acquire a computer system that's one or two steps "down" from the current top-of-the-line technology. Trace the relationship of hardware power and capacity to price, and you'll generally find a point where you must pay an unusually large price differential to buy a system at the next higher level. If you buy at a point just below where prices begin to skyrocket, you won't go too far wrong in acquiring your first computer system.

Here's a brief rundown of how the major hardware components of a computer system fit together and operate.

THE CENTRAL PROCESSOR

Often called the "heart" of the computer system, the central processor is the "chip" that controls most of the software functions you're hoping to acquire. It controls most of the hardware operations, too.

All computer software (from the start-up instructions through the operating system to the utility and application software) is written using the codes, instructions and operating procedures required by a specific type or family of central processor. Therefore, the central processor determines which software will and will not run on the computer, and you must acquire a computer with the correct central processor to support a desired software package.

Central processors of a given type can operate at different speeds, usually stated in megahertz, or millions of cycles per second. Obviously central processors that operate at faster speeds will process more data than equivalent models operating at slower speeds. But since a good deal of computer time is spent waiting for the user's next input, faster chips do not always lead to more or faster results in the office.

THE MEMORY

A computer's memory is the most important storehouse of data and instructions for the central processor. Computer memory is designed to respond to an inquiry by revealing its contents. How quickly it responds and reveals is rated as its speed, usually measured in nanoseconds (or billionths of a second). Even the slowest memory is hundreds of times faster than other types of data storage, such as disks or tapes, where responses are measured in milliseconds (or thousandths of a second). A computer's active memory may consist of one type of memory chip, or it may consist of several types of memory chips (usually there will be relatively small amounts of very fast memory and relatively large amounts of somewhat slower memory).

The computer's memory must be large enough to hold both the software instructions which the central processor is following and the data on which it is executing those instructions. As application programs get larger, computers tend to require more and more memory to support them. Today, most computers are built so that more memory can be added simply by plugging in additional memory chips.

THE DATA BACKUP/PROTECTION SYSTEM

A general rule of computers is, "If you don't want to type it in again, back it up." In practice, this means that virtually all your program and data files should be "backed up," or saved in more than one place. Some application software packages make their own backup copies of data files as you work with them. But this is rarely sufficient for complete safety of your data.

Since computer files are frequently so numerous, so carefully organized and so large, the process of adequately backing up data files can be difficult, time-consuming and tedious. That's why backup systems were invented. Backup software automates the process of copying computer files. It's possible to program the software not only to back up some or all files on a computer's hard disk or a network's file server, but to initiate the backup process automatically during the night or when people are least likely to be working with the computer.

Backup hardware provides a location—such as a high-speed tape or a disk—onto which files can be copied. Without backup hardware, you've no choice but to copy the contents of a computer's hard disk onto thirty, forty, or more floppy disks. It's no fun, which is why backup tape drives have become so popular.

THE DISPLAY

The computer's display screen is one of the most important elements in the human interface. Its size, coloration and clarity make for big differences in how easily and how well a person uses a computer. A computer's display system (screen and associated equipment) must match the requirements of particular software. Displays of particular sizes and types may also present opportunities or limitations with regard to position and glare.

At any one time, there tend to be at least two or three standards for computer displays. Software packages may require a specific one of these standards, but many packages will utilize whichever one of the display standards your computer system happens to contain.

Some display hardware can be improved with utility software. For example, laptop computers—notorious for poor-quality displays— benefit from utility software that makes the cursor easier to find and the characters larger and easier to read.

In general, there are only four hard-and-fast rules for selecting display systems:

1) Finer resolution is often easier on the eyes.
2) Larger screens are better, to a point.
3) Compared with monochrome displays, color often improves the eye's ability to distinguish shapes, patterns and groups.
4) Make sure the display you acquire supports the application software you plan to use with it.

THE KEYBOARD AND MOUSE

At this point in the development of computer technology, keyboards and mouse devices are virtual commodities. That is, there are very small or no differences between the offerings of various vendors. Keyboards and mouse devices are largely standardized for the architecture of the computer.

Certain keyboards and mouse devices have special extra keys or unusual layouts that facilitate the work you intend to do with the computer. Barring this, however, the most common basis for selecting one keyboard or mouse over another is their "feel." Some are heavier than others. Some have keys or buttons with longer travel, that is, more room to move when pressed. Various keyboards make different click sounds when pressed; others make no sound at all. Some mouse devices require a special "pad" on the desk top, others don't.

Provided you buy a keyboard or mouse from a reputable manufacturer, it should last for years. If or when it fails—and the failure of a single key or button is enough—the keyboard and mouse are two of the easiest computer components to replace. Keyboard or mouse repairs are rarely cost-effective.

THE PRINTER

For some applications, such as electronic spreadsheet modeling or simple data entry and retrieval, computers work perfectly well without a printer. But for word processing, desktop publishing and many other applications for which output to paper can be important, a printer is a useful piece of hardware.

Printers use several technologies: impact printers make marks on paper by hitting through a ribbon, like a typewriter. These are the only ones able to print on multipart forms. Nonimpact printers make marks on paper by copier-like toner transfers, or by jetting ink directly onto the page. Dot-matrix or daisy-wheel printers generally print in one small location and move the printing mechanism relative to the page to be printed. Page printers—usually employing nonimpact technology—are capable of printing everywhere on the page at one time, like a copier. Color printers use various elements from these technologies to print with combinations of primary-color inks.

Printers also differ in their paper handling capabilities. Some printers require "tractor feed" paper, the kind with holes on both sides, which it pulls through by means of special motorized pins that fit into those holes. Other printers use ordinary "cut sheets"—like letterhead or typewriter paper—which feed into the printer from one or more trays. Most printers make provision for users to feed sheets of paper or envelopes manually one at a time.

Plotters are designed to draw lines on paper—sometimes blueprint size or larger. If you are going to be working with typewriter-sized or legal-sized paper, you probably don't need a plotter.

Printer Languages

Although the printer is a self-contained piece of hardware, in operation it is connected to a host computer and steadily exchanges information with it. The exchange between a printer and a computer might be paraphrased as something like this:

Computer: Are you ready to print?
Printer: Yes, I'm ready to print.
Computer: Print this.
Printer: OK, I've printed it correctly.
Computer: Are you ready to print?
Printer: Yes, I'm ready to print.

The conversation is a trifle boring, but it gets the job done. While this example uses ordinary English, computers actually converse in specialized codes called printer control languages or page description languages. These languages use elaborate codes to communicate letters, numbers and complex graphic shapes very rapidly. Printer control languages and page description languages reside in hardware and/or software, parts of which must be installed in both the computer and the printer. If the computer and the printer are not using compatible languages, the computer cannot properly control the printer.

Some printers are designed to be connected to a single computer, others are intended to work with networks, where many different computers can send information all at the same time to be printed. If the network does not control the flow of information to the printer, the printer must be able to control the flow itself.

In evaluating printers, there are really only three considerations:

1) Does the printer produce the type of text and/or graphic output required with sufficient quality, resolution and/or color?

2) Is the printer fast enough and reliable enough to handle the quantity of output you anticipate for it, with a long enough duty cycle so it is likely to be available when needed?

3) Is the printer affordable or cost-justifiable?

THE DATA STORAGE SYSTEM

Along with the central processor and the memory, the computer's data storage system, usually a hard disk, is one of the most important components in a computer system.

The total storage capacity of the data storage system—usually measured in millions or billions of bytes—must be sufficient to contain the computer's operating system, application software, data files and what can be rather large temporary working files created as the computer operates. Its responsiveness in copying data to and from the computer's memory consists of two parts: the disk's data transfer rate is usually measured in millions of bits per second, and the disk's speed in finding data on the disk, or its "seek time," is usually measured in thousandths of a second. This responsiveness must be matched to the speed of the central processor. Too slow, and the disk becomes a bottleneck for every computer operation. Too fast, and you're paying extra for speed and a data transfer rate you can't use.

There are several different technologies for hard disk storage systems, each with different capacity ranges and data transfer speeds. All tend to be very reliable and operate for years with few if any problems. (But it's always safer to back up your data than to hope for reliability from your data storage system.) No one technology is better than another, except that more expensive systems tend to be larger and faster than less expensive ones. You will probably find it penny-wise and pound-foolish to scrimp on data storage in an otherwise fast and powerful computer system. Because newer application software tends to be much larger than previous packages, and because each task you computerize can require its own large data files and portfolio of application software, organizations that computerize tend to require a great deal more storage capacity than they first anticipate.

As a rule of thumb, you're safe to install twice as much data storage capacity as you think you will need, and smart to acquire the fastest system you can afford at that capacity. But don't make the mistake of thinking your decision on which data storage system to acquire is final. These are some of the easiest components to replace, or to supplement with additional capacity, whenever necessary.

5

Selecting Other Components

I've already covered the basic software and hardware components of a business-oriented computer system. But there are many other items you can add to the system to expand its capabilities. Here is a brief rundown on what they are, and what they do:

ATTRACTIVE TYPE FONTS

More and more computers provide the ability to print in a variety of typefaces and sizes—each of which is called a "font." It's not strictly a necessity, as printouts that mimic those from a typewriter are perfectly adequate for most purposes. But when you want to print larger spreadsheets on a single piece of paper, or create printed presentations you can hand to a customer, lender or investor, use of attractive type fonts begin to gain value.

There are several different technical systems for producing attractive type fonts on computer output. One technology requires that each font be stored separately as an independent file. If you want to print in 12 point Times Roman and 16 point Helvetica, you need both those font files on-line. If you then want to print in 14 point Times Roman, you need that file, as well.

Other font technology allows each typeface to be scaled up or down to produce virtually any point size you require. With this technology, one file of Times Roman type will allow you to print this face in any size. If you want to print in Helvetica, you need a second font file. But again, the one file will accommodate printing in virtually any point size.

The scalable font technology is more efficient in at least two respects: these font files require less disk space for storage, and they are faster to transmit from the computer to the printer. However, both systems require that the computer, the application software, and the printer are all capable of using the same technology.

DATA SECURITY

A continuing series of government and corporate investigations into the security of their computerized data shows that security measures at even the sites with the tightest securityare generally lax. What's more, few data processing managers understand how to beef up security defenses or identify which information files may already be compromised. This is a shame because virtually every company has a cache of computerized information that someone—perhaps a competitor, a criminal, a disgruntled ex-employee or a joy-riding hacker—could become motivated to explore, destroy or just alter in subtle ways. Fortunately, basic security measures are relatively easy to put in place.

The most obvious channel through which unauthorized intruders can gain access to your organization's computerized data is, of course, removable floppy disks. Secret information stored on disks can be copied or simply stolen. This can be eliminated by locking up important disks and making individuals who check them out responsible for their safe return. Innocent users can inadvertently introduce viruses and other software "bombs" into a company's computer system through the use of disks that are not searched or otherwise secured, but not if they are trained in simple security measures.

Unauthorized access to computerized data is made far easier when system administrators and users tend to ignore the password protection features readily available to them. Make your people use passwords properly, avoiding simple ones—perhaps a name or birthday—and changing them often (without writing the passwords on slips of paper they leave in a desk drawer or tape to a nearby surface). Also, remove any vendor-supplied passwords and accounts from software as soon as it is delivered. These well-known accounts and passwords constitute easily accessible "trapdoors" through which anyone who knows of them may enter.

Another major security flaw is the practice of leaving operating computers unattended, where anyone who sits down at a desk can easily attack and penetrate systems to which they have no authorized access. It's simple not to leave computers unattended. It's even simpler to install a screensaver program with a built-in password. This software automatically shuts down the computer's display and keyboard after a minute or two of inactivity, and requires a password before it will restore control to the user.

A favorite channel for intruders is commercial long-distance services, such as Tymnet or the Internet. This "dial-up" technology allows executives or sales people working from home or field offices to send and receive legitimate messages or other information without returning to headquarters. A simple security measure here is an "automatic dial-back" system. With this installed, as soon as your computer recognizes who is dialing in, it hangs up and calls back that user at a prearranged telephone number. Obviously, would-be intruders won't be at that number, and therefore cannot gain access to your system.

It's also relatively easy for system administrators or security supervisors to give each computer its own security procedures, effectively requiring multiple passwords before granting access. Each computer can also keep a well-protected history of log-on attempts and of all data file manipulations. Naturally, system administrators or security supervisors should frequently review such histories to see if hackers are making attempts to penetrate the system. In some cases, the operating system or special monitoring software can trigger a warning when a suspicious pattern occurs—such as rapid scanning of many files in directory order or wholesale copying of many unrelated data files.

ELECTRONIC MAIL

Assuming you have a reliable network or dial-up connections between two or more computers, electronic mail software can provide a quick, simple way for people to keep in close contact with each other.

With electronic mail, or e-mail, the computers take responsibility for passing messages from one user to another. The messages can be one-line questions or answers hastily typed into the computer, or elaborate files up to and including reports hundreds of pages long. Normally, your outgoing e-mail starts on the computer in your office and goes directly to the computer in your intended recipient's office. But if one or both of you happens to be traveling, the e-mail system is capable of rerouting the message as necessary, or holding the message in readiness and delivering it as soon as the recipient checks in.

There are many good electronic mail packages commercially available. Make sure the one you acquire is compatible with your network hardware and software, and that it provides the automated services and ability to route messages between as many users as you are likely to put on the system.

OTHER INPUT DEVICES

A computer's main input devices are the keyboard, the mouse and electronic transfers of information from disks, over networks and through dial-up connections. This will take care of the vast majority of requirements for most business applications. But there are a great many other ways to provide a computer with more specialized information and input.

For example, the most common ways to move a computer's cursor around the screen and through a data file have always been a set of four arrow keys that control cursor movement in one of the cardinal directions. More recently, the hand-held "mouse" has become something of a standard. But over the years, engineers have come up with a variety of alternative "pointing devices" that promise a range of choices, if not better performance. These alternatives include cordless and other advanced mice, trackballs, mouse pens, various implementations of touch screens, light pens, "isopoints" and joysticks. Most of these will work with most applications, but it's important to try a pointing device with your favorite software not only to see if you like it, but to be sure they're compatible.

Cordless and Other Advanced Mice
An interesting advance over the standard mouse is the development of different mouse configurations, including larger than normal sizes, and left-handed or right-handed designs. This approach not only provides more comfort for the mouse user, but effectively ends the electronic update to the old-fashioned practice of forcing lefties to work with their right hands. Another advance, though not so important for most applications, is the replacement of the mouse's tangle-prone cord with infrared or low-power radio technology.

Trackballs
A trackball can be thought of as an upside-down mouse. It's a box with a ball in it. As you spin the ball a given distance in a given direction, the cursor moves accordingly. One advantage of this arrangement is that the whole device stays in one place on your desk. The most convenient trackball designs let the fingers fall naturally on both the ball and the buttons. There are relatively small trackball units that clip to the side of laptop computers, the smallest being about the size of a marble. Several keyboards have trackballs built right in, and more keyboards will certainly provide this option in years to come.

Mouse Pens

The mouse pen is a mouse on the end of a pen-like stick, with buttons placed strategically on the barrel of the pen. To use it, you simply grasp the mouse pen like any pen, and "write" with it on any convenient surface. The computer senses the mouse pen's movement and causes the cursor to mimic that movement. The advantage of this design is that you use muscles already trained to write, automatically minimizing fatigue and improving precision.

Isopoints

The "isopoint" combines a rotating rod with a sliding pointer. The slider provides left-right cursor movement, while rod rotation moves the cursor up or down on the screen. This device combines the advantages of the trackball with the tactile feel and feedback of the more common mouse, and can be built right into the keyboard.

Joysticks

Joysticks function like the control stick in an airplane. Small ones can be positioned right next to the keyboard for easy, variable speed cursor movement and mouse emulation. These devices are convenient and easy to use, but may not provide for the precise positioning of the cursor any better than an ordinary mouse or trackball.

Touch Screens

Touch screens have been available for many years. Most operate with touch-sensitive mesh in front of the screen, or a series of lights arrayed in a grid around the screen so that anything touching it blocks several of the light beams, or a screen that electronically "senses" where a finger touches it. Although all the hardware is built in and responds to your natural pointing actions with no thought on your part, the average finger is too large to point as precisely as one might want. Also, some touch screens are incompatible with your favorite software.

A different kind of touch screen lies flat next to the keyboard and operates in several different ways. The device can emulate a trackball or a mouse, but in "absolute" mode, you can touch the screen anywhere and the cursor instantly travels to that point.

Light Pens

The "light pen" is a combination of the mouse pen and the touch screen. Instead of touching the screen with your finger, you touch it with the light pen. These devices have been around for years, and have proven to be very convenient and effective in expensive applications like video-editing and interactive education systems.

Digitizers

This is a device to convert a drawing, graphic or other two-dimensional material into the digital form a computer can manipulate. Digitizers were once mechanical devices primarily intended to trace the outlines of pictures. Today, these have been replaced by electronic scanners, and digitizing has begun to adapt to audio, video and other forms of information.

Scanners

The scanner is a modern form of digitizer that converts a printed photograph, drawing or text into an electronic image the computer can store, manipulate and later reprint. Some scanners can perceive only shades of gray, while others can perceive color. Some are hand-held, and must be passed over the material to be scanned, while others—generally the more expensive and more accurate ones—provide a glass "bed" on which you place the material to be scanned.

For the computer to operate the scanner, it requires special software. This software not only causes the scanner to process the printed material, it then offers a variety of capabilities for manipulating the image. These capabilities allow you to cut, paste, save, retrieve and modify the image in various ways. However, a scanned image of text is not the same as text. That is, the computer may be able to capture and manipulate the image of the word *Apple*, but it cannot sort that image into alphabetical order with other images of words, change it to the image of the word *Ball* or check it for spelling. To edit a scanned image of text in any of these ways, the computer must first convert it from image to text. This is done by optical character recognition (OCR) software.

Data Gathering Devices

Computers can be fitted with a wide variety of sensors that feed information directly into the processor, for use primarily in laboratories, scientific and manufacturing applications. This is a highly complex area well beyond the scope of this book. But if you need such an application, it's certainly available. Contact computer consultants or suppliers in your field for more information.

OTHER OUTPUT DEVICES

Aside from printers and display screens, the computer can operate a wide variety of data output devices. Depending on what you want the computer to accomplish, you can generally attach these devices and the special software each one requires in any combination you may wish.

Audio
For a long time computers have had small, single speakers through which they could beep, honk, and make other attention-getting noises. But in recent years, the trend has been to provide them with full audio capabilities. This, coupled with improved digital recording of audio information now gives computers the potential to play music, annotate documents with your recorded voice and create sound effects or synthesized sounds.

Audio capabilities are an important part of the "multimedia" computer. This is a highly specialized area that not only requires special-purpose hardware and software, but also needs people who have the imagination and training to figure out how to use these capabilities.

Video
As with audio, computers are rapidly gaining control over television pictures. Complete editing, titling and special-effects systems are now delivered within relatively inexpensive personal computers. Just as word processors and desktop publishing placed professional-quality print materials within reach of every small business, computerized video systems are placing professional-quality television productions within reach of the same large pool of users.

Slides and Transparencies
Desktop publishing and presentation software have made it easy to produce high quality printed materials for distribution at important meetings and seminars, or for general publication. One added feature of these sys-

tems is the ability to convert the printed output to slides and/or transparencies.

In general, it requires software to translate the file intended for printing into a slightly different file intended for slides. It also requires the appropriate hardware to transfer this information onto film rather than paper.

Since few organizations have much call for this capability, there are a number of service bureaus that produce visual materials from standardized files. You send them the file and they send you the slides or transparencies by return mail. The vendors who provide software with the requisite capabilities can generally put you in touch with one or more of these service bureaus.

Machine Control

Large computers have been operating machines for years. But recently, personal computers have also been adapted for machine control by the installation of specialized hardware boards that operate specific motors and electronic switches fitted to the machines to be controlled.

The most common applications for machine control by personal computers are heating, ventilating, lighting, air conditioning and fire safety systems in homes and other buildings.

Plotters

This is a computer printer specially designed to draw lines on very large sheets of paper, mainly for blueprints and similar applications. Plotters frequently use a set of specialized pens to draw their lines. Page printers can do some plotting, but with their letter-sized or legal-sized paper handling capacities, they are not well-designed for producing very large-scale output.

The Data Modem

The data modem is an electronic device that, when sending, converts a computer's tiny digital signals into audible sounds that a standard telephone line can carry successfully, and reverses the process when receiving. Two computers equipped with compatible modems can thus exchange information over an ordinary telephone line. Modern data modems are very well standardized. For convenience, they can usually dial and answer the telephone on their own, allowing the communicating computers to make connections automatically. Since the data modem is a hardware device, the computer requires special software in order to be able to operate it. Most communications packages go beyond the basics of controlling the modem and offer capabilities to:

• store frequently used telephone numbers,
• provide automatic features so you can leave your computer unattended and allow others to call up and exchange files with it, or
• automatically call and connect with computers you communicate with frequently.

Some communications software and data modems also include standardized methods to encode and decode files to be transmitted, and to verify that a file has been received accurately.

The main difference between various data modems that meet established standards is the speed at which they can send and receive information. Clearly, the faster the transfer rate, the less time it takes to send or receive a given quantity of information. 300 BAUD is considered very slow. 1200 BAUD (four times faster) is close to an average person's normal reading speed. 2400 BAUD is obviously twice as fast as normal reading speed. Modems are available at 9600 BAUD, 14,400 BAUD, 19,200 BAUD, and beyond. But prices for faster modems tend to go up precipitously.

The Fax Modem

A facsimile (or fax) machine incorporates both a scanner and a printer. The information transmitted by fax is an image of the material scanned. Adding a fax modem to your computer allows it to send or receive these fax images just like a standard fax machine. But the images remain inside your computer where they can be manipulated and controlled by other software. Unlike regular text files or other data files generated by your applications, image files are fixed, like a photo, and remain unintelligible to word processors, electronic spreadsheets, database managers and other applications unless converted from image to text. In order to edit material received by your computer's fax modem, the image file must be processed by OCR software and converted to text. Similarly, to send a text file out through your fax modem, you must first reverse the OCR process and convert the text to an image file.

THE NETWORK

Networks are among the most complicated components of any computer system. They are made up of many "layers" of software and associated hardware, all of which must be fully compatible and properly installed for the network to operate successfully. Although vendors are steadily making networks simpler to install and manage, it's advisable that you get help before you invest in your first network.

Local Area Networks (LANs) are primarily used within a department or work group, or within a single floor of a building or a relatively small geographical area. The LAN connects all the designated computers together so they can exchange e-mail, utilize printers and other resources in common, and share access to the same data and program files.

Wide Area Networks (WANs) generally encompass far larger geographical areas, perhaps a town, a county, a state, or even an entire country. Within that area, all the designated computers (normally those of the company or government agency setting up the WAN) are connected the same as they would be on a LAN.

The differences between a LAN and a WAN are largely technical. In well-designed networks, the user sees little or no difference in connectivity, and may not even know—or need to know—the network configuration. Here's a brief rundown of the major parts of a network:

Network Operating System

This is like the operating system of a stand-alone computer. It controls and manages the activity of all the parts of the network, particularly storage and other resources. Network software, utilities and hardware must all be compatible with the network operating system.

Network File Server

Most computer networks provide a central repository for data files and program files that any user can access over the network. This is the file server. It generally consists of a relatively large, relatively fast disk storage system and appropriate software to let many different computers access it simultaneously. Often, the file server is part of the same computer on which the network operating system resides.

Hubs, Bridges and Routers

In general, you can visualize a network as a hallway or a series of hallways along which people shout brief messages. Obviously, if more than one person is shouting at the same time, all the messages become garbled. Since everyone waits for everyone else's messages to pass along the network, it's very easy for the network to slow down as the amount of traffic builds up. That's one of the main reasons hubs, bridges and routers are used. These devices tend to close doors between the hallways, effectively creating many sub-networks and confining each message to the fewest and shortest hallways actually required for it to reach its destination. This tends to reduce traffic on other parts of the network, thus reducing the average delay for every message on the network.

Wireless Networks

Until recently, all networks required a wire directly connected to each and every computer that would be communicating. However, wires are expensive to install and expensive to move as people and their computers are shuffled around within a building or on a campus.

Wireless networks operate by two-way radio waves or infrared light, and therefore do not require each computer to be wired in. You can move one of these computers anywhere within the field of wireless connectivity, and it remains part of the network. Another form of wireless network is one-way transmission of information, news, stock quotes or the like—out to people using computers anywhere in a campus, city, state or country.

VOICE MAIL

This is a capability built into a hardware device that connects a computer to telephone lines. Usually packaged with its own software, the device can be programmed to answer the telephone, deliver a recorded message or menu of messages, and record each caller's message. Various voice mail devices can store these messages protected by each authorized user's personal identification number, and play them back when requested to do so. They can also add a user's voice notes to a message and forward the combination to another authorized user. Voice mail devices can also be used to record a message and deliver it—via telephone—to any number of people whose names and numbers are contained in an accompanying data file.

OTHER SOFTWARE

Aside from the most common and generic software, discussed in detail in Chapter 3, there are many other types of more specialized, limited-purpose applications you can use. Here is a brief description of these additional computer capabilities:

Personal Phone Books

These are special-purpose database programs designed to store a large number of names and telephone numbers, retrieve the one you want, and automatically dial it (provided the computer contains a compatible data modem).

Schedulers or Appointment Books

These are special-purpose database programs preprogrammed with the days and dates for years into the future. Users can list upcoming appointments in these databases, and later use the software to look at their schedule for a day, a week or a month. Appointments can be reviewed, shifted to another day or time, or set to repeat automatically. When used over a network for a group of people, interoffice meetings can be scheduled by the computer at times when all the attendees are not previously engaged.

Contact Managers

These are special-purpose database programs that generally include a scheduler, a note pad or word processor, and a personal telephone book. You record pertinent information about the people you contact, appointments you have with them, and any information and promises you may have exchanged. The idea is for this software to augment your memory and make it easier to keep up business-oriented relationships with a large number of people.

Utilities

Clearly, a computer system is a complex tool for business. Various types of utility software packages have been developed to simplify the task of managing and working with the computer system itself and the information it contains. Here is a brief rundown of the main types of utility software:

Disk Utilities

These are intended for working with the files on your computer's hard disk storage system. File management utilities allow you to look at, copy, move, rename or delete any or all of the files on your disk. This is important as you can easily have several thousand program and data files. These utilities provide a simple way to delete the clutter of unnecessary data file backups made automatically by various programs. They also help you find data files you know you stored but cannot locate because you have forgotten where you put them or what you named them.

Optimizing utilities allow you to fine-tune your disk for faster, safer performance. These utilities can rearrange files on the disk so the ones you access most often are placed where they can be found most quickly, and can modify the storage patterns on your disk to improve overall performance. They can also combine the fragments of a data file, stored in several locations, into a single, contiguous file the computer can retrieve more quickly.

Keyboard Utilities

Keyboard macro programs allow you to program individual keys or two-key combinations with virtually any sequence of characters and/or computer commands you wish. Some word processing, spreadsheet and other application programs have such macro capabilities built in. But others do not, so keyboard utilities allow you to add them when and where you wish. Other keyboard utilities modify how the keyboard operates, including such details as how quickly a key you hold down repeats itself.

Screen Utilities

These small software packages modify how your computer makes use of the display screen. For laptops, screen utilities exist to make the cursor far easier to see and the contrast between background and foreground much sharper. Some can also modify the font used for screen display so the letters and numbers are easier to read.

For many computers, screen utilities have been developed to display 43 lines of text or more, rather than the usual 25 lines. It's also possible (on a color display) to assign any color you like to the text, the background, the borders and so forth.

Printer Utilities
The most useful printer utilities create a buffer (or temporary memory space) between application programs and the printer. The immediate advantage is that the user regains control over the computer much faster than if the application program waited for the much slower printer to finish processing its output. In addition, the printer utility may allow the user a great deal of control over the contents of the printer buffer, such as the ability to print several copies, to print individual pages, to zoom the printed material down in size so four pages will print in the space normally used for one, or to convert bitmapped output so it can be used with vector-graphics or scalable-graphics printers.

Cache Utilities
A cache (like a buffer) provides a temporary memory location in which the computer stores data moving within the system. The cache is generally much faster than other computer memory locations, and this special software actively controls the flow of information into and out of the cache. A *disk* cache stores data flowing between the computer's hard disk and its memory, attempting to anticipate the information the processor might ask for next and also combining many small disk access operations into fewer, more efficient ones. If the processor asks for information already in the cache, the disk does not even come into play. A disk cache greatly improves performance for database work and other applications where the computer accesses the disk frequently. Today's most modern disk controller boards have small disk caches built in.

A *memory* cache stores data flowing between the computer's memory and the processor. If the next request is for information already in the cache, it flows to the processor much faster than it would from the computer's ordinary active memory. A memory cache greatly improves performance in almost all computer operations. Today's most modern processor chips have small memory caches built in.

Diagnostic/Recovery Utilities

Because computer systems are so complex, an error or malfunction anywhere can create strange problems that are difficult to diagnose. *Diagnostic* utilities examine all the components of a computer system and identify those that do not meet established specifications. If the computer system fails completely, obviously you won't be able to use a diagnostic utility. But if there is a partial breakdown, a diagnostic utility may help pinpoint the cause of it.

Recovery utilities are applied to computer hard disks that lose or scramble data. Even if the entire disk malfunctions, the problem may be due to a tiny problem in the disk's internal software. Recovery software can sometimes find this problem and repair it, miraculously bringing the disk "back to life."

If the problem is with some or all of the files on the disk, other types of recovery utilities can attempt to reconstruct the files and make them accessible to your applications once again.

Efficiency Utilities

Not for the fainthearted, these software packages allow you to modify many of the internal adjustments, settings and commands within the computer system that control how it uses memory and other resources. Since the wrong setting or adjustment can render the computer entirely inoperative, it's best to leave this software for the experts.

Software for Education and Training

Many applications come with tutorials that allow the new user to learn the basics of how to operate the software. Try one, and you'll get a taste of computerized education and training.

Education and training software can provide students or trainees with a particular series of experiences through the computer's display and other devices. Or the software can be generic—like word processing or an electronic spreadsheet—and provide a means for you to create any education and training experiences you wish.

In recent years, the advent of software that allows computers to control videodiscs, touch screens and multimedia devices has created the potential for sophisticated education and training systems that adjust automatically to individual students. The software can ask some fundamental questions, and use a student's responses as the basis for choosing what to teach that student next.

Aids to Word Processing
A variety of utilities exists to improve upon the basic features of word processing software. Some of these utilities are incorporated in some word processing packages. Others remain as "add-ons" you must purchase separately and install.

Grammar-Checking Utilities
These utilities let the computer analyze the words in your written material to find errors and suggest improvements. Most grammar-checkers allow you to set them for very strict adherence to grammatical rules (suitable for academic or technical writing) or very loose interpretation of rules (appropriate for fiction or general letter writing). Most business people will find a comfortable mid-level setting that catches egregious errors without insisting on more review and rewriting than you can put up with. Advanced grammar-checkers will examine your use of slang, acronyms and foreign words, and will comment on your choice of words, sentence length and construction.

Dictionaries and Thesaurus
The primary use of a computerized dictionary is to check the spelling of the words in your document. But the same computerized dictionary required for spell-checking can also support more sophisticated features, such as a thesaurus capability that will show you lists of words having very similar—or nearly opposite—meanings to any word you've highlighted in your document. Select the one you want and it instantly replaces the highlighted word.

On-line dictionaries give you the meanings of a word you highlight in your document. A few operate in reverse. That is, you specify a few words for a meaning, and the dictionary shows you all the words with definitions containing your specifications. This comes in handy when you're trying to think of the name of a particular product or tool, or the name for a certain concept used frequently in accounting.

Ready-Made Letters
One of the simplest ways to improve your writing is to obtain copies of prewritten business letters. By selecting the proper letter and loading it

into your word processor, you start with a solid basis for each of your most common writing chores. Then you simply add the appropriate details and make the appropriate changes or deletions to "make the letter your own." Because you started with a good letter, you'll finish your writing much faster and easier than if you had started from scratch.

Outlining
One of the most important improvements to ordinary word processors is the addition of an "outlining" capability. This harnesses the power of the computer to help you organize, reorganize and present information—in anything from a business plan to a daily memo—far more quickly and easily than you could without it. In addition, many outliners contain sorting routines, so long lists can be reshuffled as necessary for easy reference.

CAD / Drawing / Paint Programs
Computer Aided Design (CAD) software, or its more generic, less capable drawing or painting software relatives, gives the computer the ability to draw and edit shapes on the display screen and a suitable printer. Such software can be used by product designers, engineers, and/or manufacturing specialists to do their drawings and computations more quickly and easily than they could directly on paper.

DESKTOP PUBLISHING

Beyond word processing, computer software can provide a range of precision formatting and printing controls that together are called "desktop publishing." These desktop publishers make it easy to incorporate both text and graphics into a document. This means dry reports and memos can be dressed up with charts, graphs, logos, and other visual emphatics. Multicolumn capabilities eliminate the difficulties of making tables and similar presentations of data. They also speed preparation of newsletters and other finished materials to be printed.

DATA BACKUP

Because information stored in a computer can be damaged or destroyed at any time, it's always a good policy to keep a second and perhaps even a third copy of important files. Making these "backup" copies can become tedious, which is why many people prefer to use special software and hardware devices for this process.

Hardware devices for creating "backup" copies can use either disks or tapes. You can back up to floppy disks, but for a 40 MB (mega-byte) hard disk or larger this takes quite a long time and requires changing floppies a dozen or several dozen times. It's easier to back up to a high speed tape device. Since one tape can easily hold 250 MB or more, there's no need to stay around during the copying process. It's also possible to install two hard drives in a computer and "back up" your data by copying information from one disk to another. Obviously, "backup" software automates the copying process, which can even be completed at a preset time, such as after regular business hours.

Few computers contain all these hardware and software capabilities. There's no need, particularly since each one costs money and you can add a feature whenever you really need it. So pick and choose carefully, based on your estimates of your business' present requirements, and you'll enjoy long years of productive, cost-effective service from your business computer system.

6

Resources

HARDWARE AND SOFTWARE VENDORS

Here is a selected list of hardware and software vendors whose products you might want to explore. Naturally, you can get the names, addresses, and telephone numbers of any vendors not on this list from your local computer retailers or libraries, or from computer magazines.

Abaton/Everex
48431 Milmont Drive
Fremont, CA 94538
800-444-5321

Acer Technologies Corp.
401 Charcot Ave.
San Jose, CA 95131
408-922-0333

Action Technologies
1301 Marina Village Pkwy.
Alameda, CA 94501
510-521-6190

Adaptec, Inc.
691 S. Milpitas Blvd.
Milpitas, CA 95035
408-945-8600

Adobe Systems
1870 BM Darcadero Rd.
Palo Alto, CA 94303
800-292-3623

Affinity Microsystems
1050 Walnut St.
Suite
Boulder, CO 80302
800-367-6771

AGFA Intel. Font
90 Industrial Way
Wilmington, MA 01887
800-873-3668

Aldus
411 First Ave. S. 200
Seattle, WA 98104
206-628-2320

All Computers
21 St. Claire Ave. E
Suite 203
Toronto, ON CD M4T IL9
800-387-2744

Alloy Computer Products
165 Forest St.
Marlboro, MA 01752
800-326-7836

Alpha Software
30 B St.
Burlington, MA 01803
617-229-2924

ANSA Software
13455 Noel Rd.
Suite 1670
Dallas, TX 75240
214-960-1748

Apple Computers
20525 Mariani Ave.
Cupertino, CA 95014
800-282-2732

Archive Corp.
1650 Sunflower Ave.
Costa Mesa, CA 92626
714-641-0279

Artisoft, Inc.
3550 N. 1st Ave.
Tucson, AZ 85719
602-293-6363

Ask Sam Software
PO Box 1428
Perry, FL 32347
800-327-5726

AST Research
16215 Alton Pkwy.
Irvine, CA 92713-9658
800-723-2278

AT&T Info Systems
225 Littleton Rd.
Morris Plains, NJ 07950
201-631-1443

Autodesk
2320 Marinship Way
Sausalito, CA 94965
415-331-0356

Banyan Vines (Systems)
120 Flanders Rd.
Westboro, MA 01581
214-746-3311

Basic Computers
1585 Frederick
Akron, OH
216-873-1000

BLOC Publishing
1301 Dade Blvd.
Miami Beach, FL
305-531-5486

Blue Sky Software
7486 La Jolla Blvd.
La Jolla, CA 92037
800-677-4946

Boeing Computer Services
2810 - 106th Ave. S.E.
Bellevue, WA 98008
206-644-6544

Boffin Industries
2500 West County Rd. - 42
Burnsville, MN 55237
612-894-0595

Borland Int'l.
4585 Scotts Valley Dr.
Scotts Valley, CA 95066
408-461-9000

Bourbaki, Inc.
PO Box 2867
Boise, ID 83701
208-342-5849

Brightbill Roberts
120 E. Washington #421
Syracuse, NY 13202
315-474-3400

Broderbund
1938 Fourth St.
San Rafael, CA 94901
415-479-1700

Brown Bag Software
2105 S. Bascom
Suite 164
Campbell, CA 95008
800-523-0764

Budget Computer, Inc.
8745 E. Orchard Rd.
Englewood, CO 80111
303-741-4505

Buttonware
11058 Main St.
Bellevue, WA 98004
206-454-0479

C.Itoh
19300 S Hamilton Ave.
Suite 110
Torrance, CA 90508
800-347-4840

CalComp
2411 W. La Palma
Anaheim, CA 92803
800-225-2667

Calera Recognition Systems
2500 Augustine Dr.
Santa Clara, CA 95054
408-986-8006

Cambridge Software
80 Mt. Sandford Rd.
Mt. Carmel, CT 06518
800-462-4481

Canon USA
3200 Regent Blvd.
Irving, TX 75063
214-830-9600

Centel Info Systems
11400 Commerce Park Dr.
Reston, VA 22091
703-758-7102

Chinon America, Inc.
660 Maple Ave.
Torrance, CA 90503
800-441-0222

Citadel Systems
PO Box 7219
The Woodlands, TX 77387-7219
713-363-2384

Clarion Software
150 E Sample Rd.
Pompano Beach, CA 33064
800-354-5444

Codex
7 Blue Hill River Rd.
Canton, MA 02021
800-426-1212

COMP USA
15182 Marsh Lane
Dallas, TX 75243
214-406-4700

Compaq Computer Corp.
14902 Sommermeyer
Houston, TX 77041
800-231-9977

Compugraphics
90 Industrial Way
Wilmington, MA 01887
800-424-8973

Computer Associates Intl
101 North Wacker Dr.
Chicago, IL 60606
312-201-6117

Computer Peripherals
667 Rancho Conego Blvd.
Newbury Park, CA 91320
800-854-7600

Control Data
9315 Largo Drive West
Landover, MD 20785-4755
301-808-4270

Corel Systems
1600 Carling Ave.
Ottowa Ontario, Can K1Z-8R7

Corvus Systems, Inc.
160 Great Oaks Blvd.
San Jose, CA 95119
800-426-7887

Cougar Mountain Software
2609 Kootenai
Boise, ID 83705
800-344-2540

CSCI
4849 Ronson Ct. #101
San Diego, CA 92111
619-571-7156

CXI Incorporated
4801 Woodway Dr. #300E
Houston, TX 77056
713-622-6935

Cybertek, Inc.
6133 Bristol Pkwy. #300
Culver City, CA 90230
213-649-2450

Cybex
2800-H Bob Wallace Ave.
Huntsville, AL 35805
205-534-0011

Cyma McGraw-Hill
2530 S Parker Rd. #209
Aurora, CO 80014
800-292-2962

Data Desk International
7651 Haskell Ave.
Van Nuys, CA 91406
800-826-5398

Data Link, Inc.
890 N Dorothy Dr.
Suite 906
Richardson, TX 75081
214-644-6112

Dataproducts
999 Old Eagle School Rd.
Wayne, PA 19087
800-334-3174

Decision Support Systems
8250-B Tyco Rd.
Vienna, VA 22180
800-231-4279

Delrina Technology
6830 Via Del Oro
San Jose, CA 95119
800-268-6082

Digital Research
60 Garden Court
Monterey, CA 93942
408-649-3896

Electronic Arts
1820 Gateway Dr.
San Mateo, CA 94404
415-571-7171

Epson America
1950 Stemmons Frwy. 2029
Dallas, TX 75207
800-234-1445

Everex Systems, Inc.
48346 Milmont Dr.
Bldg. 4
Fremont, CA 94538
800-821-0806
800-356-4283

Excelan
2180 Fortune Dr.
San Jose, CA 95131
800-392-3526

Fifth Generation
10049 N. Reiger Rd.
Baton Rouge, LA 70809
504-291-7221

Formworx
1601 Trapelo Rd.
Waltham, MA 02154
800-992-0085

Fox & Geller
604 Market St.
Elmwood Park, NJ 07407
201-794-8883

Frontline Systems
PO Box 2001
Cameron Park, CA 95682
4153-277-297

Fujitsu
3055 Orchid Dr.
San Jose, CA 95134-2022
800-233-1798

Gazelle, Inc.
42 N. University Ave. 10
Provo, UT 84601
800-233-0383

Goldenbow Sytems
2870 5th Ave.
Suite 201
San Diego, CA 92103
619-298-9349

Grid Systems
115 North Charles St.
Baltimore, MD 21201
800-356-4743

Hauppauge Computer Works
91 Cabot Court
Hauppauge, NY 11788
516-434-1600

Hewlett Packard
PO Box 152030
Irving, TX 75085
800-822-4772

IBM Entry Systems Div.
2005 Market St.
Philadelphia, PA 19103
215-851-3491

IBM National Parts Center
PO Box 12883 Dept. N06
Lexington, KY 40583
606-232-5902

Indigo Software
2755 Campus Dr.
San Mateo, CA 94403
415-312-0770

Information Builders, Inc.
5420 LBJ Freeway #1830
Dallas, TX
800-848-8683

Informix, Inc.
51 West Mill St.
Medfield, MA
617-359-5378

Ingram Micro, Inc.
3301 W. Segerstrom
Santa Anna, CA 92704
800-456-8000

Innovative Software
1142 Chess Dr.
Foster City, CA 94404
415-570-5967

Intel Corporation
5200 N E Elam Young Pkwy.
Hillsboro, OR 97124
503-629-7423

Intellicom
9259 Eton Ave.
Chatsworth, CA 91311
818-407-3900

Intelligent Devices
112 Harvard St.
Clairmont, CA 91711
714-920-9551

Intuit
540 University Ave.
Palo Alto, CA 94301
415-322-0573

Invisible Software
1165 Chess Drive Suite D
Foster City, CA 94404
415-570-5967

Iomega
5501 LBJ Frwy., Suite 500
Dallas, TX 75240
801-778-1000

Jameco
1355 Shore Way Rd.
Belmont, CA 94002
415-592-8097

Keytronics
North 4424 Sullivan Rd.
Spokane, WA 99214
800-262-6006

Knowledge Dynamics
Box 1558
Canyon Lake, TX 78130-1558
800-331-2783

Kyocera Unison, Inc.
1321 Harbor Bay Pkwy.
Alameda, CA 94501
510-748-6680

Lantana Technology, Inc.
4393 Viewridge Ave.
Suite A
San Diego, CA 92123
800-666-4526

Lasertools Corp.
5900 Hollis St.
Emeryville, CA 94608
510-420-8777

Leading Edge Software
21 Highland Circle
Needham, MA 021994
617-449-4655

Logitech, Inc.
6505 Kaiser Dr.
Fremont, CA 94555
510-713-4617

Lotus Development
55 Cambridge Pkwy.
Cambridge, MA 02142
800-828-6693

Macromind
410 Townsend
Suite 408
San Francisco, CA 94107
415-442-0200

Mannesmann Tally
8301 S. 180th St.
Kent, WA 98032-0413
214-669-2984

Maxthink
3718 Grand Ave.
Oakland, CA 94610
415-428-0104

Maxtor
2191 Zanker Rd.
San Jose, CA 95134
214-241-1025

Maynard
36 Skyline Dr.
Lake Mary, FL 32746
407-263-3461

Microcom
5001 Spring Valley #400E
Dallas, TX 75244
800-552-3245

Microdyne
3601 Eisenhower Ave.
Alexandria, VA 22304
703-329-3700

Micrografx, Inc.
1303 E Arapaho Rd.
Richardson, TX 75081
214-234-1769

Micrologic
PO Box 174
Hackensack, NJ 07602
201-342-6518

Micropolis Corp.
21123 Nordhoff St.
Chatsworth, CA 91311
818-709-3300

Micropro
14800 Quorum Dr. #345
Dallas, TX 75240
214-980-7232

Microrim
3925 159th Ave. NE
Redmond, WA 98052
800-248-2001

Microsoft
1 Microsoft Way
Redmond, WA 98052
800-227-4679

Microspeed
5307 Randolph Place
Fremont, CA 94538
415-490-1403

Miniscribe
9330 LBJ Fwy. #900
Dallas, TX 75243
800-356-5333

Mountain Computer, Inc.
360 El Pueblo Rd.
Scotts Valley, CA 95066
800-243-8188

Mouse Systems
47505 Seabridge Dr.
Freemont, CA 94538
510-656-1117

Multisoft Corp.
18220 SW Monte Verdi Blvd.
Beaverton, OR 97007
503-642-7108

Mylex
47650 Westinghouse Dr.
Fremont, CA 94539
800-446-9539

NCR
2301 Research Blvd.
Rockville, MD 20850
301-258-6750

NEC Home Electronics
1020 Frontenac Rd.
Naperville, IL 60563
312-860-5739

NEC Technologies, Inc.
13355 Noel Rd.
Suite 300
Dallas, TX 75240
214-385-8384

Next Wave Software
1800 Water Pl.
Suite 280
Atlanta, GA 30339
404-422-8255

Nexus
8535 Cliff Cameron Dr. #1
Charlotte, NC 28269
704-549-9444

Northgate Computer System
13895 Industrial Park #110
Plymouth, MN 55441
612-943-8181

Novell
122 E 1700 South
Provo, UT 84601
801-429-5621

OCR Systems
1800 Byberry Rd.
Huntingdon Valley, PA 19006
800-233-4627

Officeworks
3402-H West Wendover Park
Greensboro, NC 27417
717-397-7766

Oracle Corp.
20 Davis Dr.
Belmont, CA 94002
415-506-3839

Orchid Technologies
47790 Westinghouse Dr.
Fremont, CA 94539
800-767-2443

Pacific Data Products
9125 Rehco Rd.
San Diego, CA 92121
619-597-3320

Packard Bell
9425 Canoga Ave.
Chatsworth, CA 91311
510-831-4805

Paperback Software
2830 Ninth St.
Berkeley, CA 94710
415-644-2116

Patton & Patton
485 Cochrane Circle
Morgan Hill, CA 95037
408-778-6557

Perceptive Solutions, Inc.
2700 Flora
Dallas, TX 75201
800-486-3278

Pergamon Software
Maxwell House, Fairvew Pk.
Elmsford, NY 10523
914-592-7700

Peter Norton Computing Co.
2210 Wilshire Blvd. #186
Santa Monica, CA 90403
213-453-2361

Pharlap Software
60 Aberdeen Ave.
Cambridge, MA 02138
617-661-1510

PK Ware, Inc.
9025 N. Deerwood Dr.
Brown Deer, WI 53223
414-354-8699

Poquet Computer Corp
650 N Mary Ave.
Sunnyvale, CA 94086
708-490-5349

Portable Solutions
1701 Directors Blvd. St250
Austin, TX 78744
512-448-4965

Practical Peripherals, Inc.
31245 La Baya Dr.
Westlake Village, CA 91362
818-706-0333

Printronix, Inc.
17500 Cartwright Rd.
Irvine, CA 92713
800-826-3874

Qualitas
7101 Wisconsin Ave.
Bethesda, MD 20814-4805
301-907-6700

Quarterdeck
150 West Pico Blvd.
Santa Monica, CA 90405
310-392-9851

QUBIE
507 Calle San Pablo
Camarillo, CA 93010

Quicksoft
219 First Ave. A. #224
Seattle, WA 98109
206-282-0452

Racal Vadic
1601 N. Harrison Pkwy.
Sunrise, FL 33323
800-333-4143

Radio Shack
312 Medallion
Dallas, TX 75214
214-363-4628

Radius, Inc.
1710 Fortune Dr.
San Jose, CA 95131
408-954-6866

Ricoh (Daisytek)
10440 Markson Rd.
Dallas, TX 75238
800-527-4212

Samna Corp.
5470 Oakbrook Pkwy.
Norcross, GA 30093
404-448-5241

Scitor Corp.
393 Vintage Park Dr. #140
Foster City, CA 94404
415-570-7700

Sears Business Centers
Sears Tower
Chicago, IL 60684
312-875-0336

Sensible Software
335 East Big Beaver Suite
Troy, MI 48083
313-528-1950

Sharp Systems
2320 E St.
La Verne, CA 91750
714-596-0070

Softcorp, Inc.
2340 State Rd. 580 #244
Clearwater, FL 33575
813-799-3984

Softklone
1210 E. Park Ave.
Tallahassee, FL 32301
904-878-8564

Softlogic Solutions
530 Chestnut St.
Manchester, NH 03101
603-627-9900

Software Architects, Inc.
11812 N Creek Pkwy., N. St.
Bothell, WA 98011
206-487-0122

Software Publishing
P.O. Box 54983
Santa Clara, CA 95056-0983
214-985-4044

Solution Systems, Inc.
541 Main St.. Suite 410
South Weymouth, MA 02190
800-821-2492

Solutions Systems
3721 Washington St.
Wellesley, MA 02181
800-821-2492

Sony Corp. Of America
Sony Dr.
Park Ridge, NJ 07656
201-930-7669

Spinnaker/Hayden
One Kendall Square
Cambridge, MA 02139
617-494-1200

SRI International
Network Info Center
Menlo Park, CA 94015
415-859-6387

STAC Electronics
5993 Avenida Encinas
Carlsbad, CA 92008
800-522-7822

STB Systems
601 N. Glenville Dr.
Richardson, TX 75081
214-234-8750

Storage Dimensions
1656 Mccarthy Blvd.
Milpitas, CA 95035
408-894-1448

Sun Computers
1952 Jerricho Turnpike
East Northport, NY 11731
516-462-6700

Symantec Corporation
10201 Torre Ave.
Cupertino, CA 95014
800-222-2616

Tall Tree Systems
2585 East Bayshore Rd.
Palo Alto, CA 94303
415-493-1980

Tallgrass Technologies
11100 W. 82nd St.
Overland Park, KS 66214
800-736-6002

Tandon Corporation
609 Science Dr.
Moorpark, CA 93021
805-378-3075

Tangent Technologies
5720 Peachtree Pkwy. 100
Norcross, GA 30092
404-662-0366

Tektronix, Inc.
11814 115th Ave. N.E.
Kirkland, WA 98034
800-835-6100

Timeslips Corporation
239 Western Ave.
Essex, MA 01929
800-338-5314

Toshiba America
9740 Irvine Blvd.
Irvine, CA 92713
800-627-1273

Turner-Hall Publishing Co.
10201 Torre Ave.
Cupertino, CA 95014
800-556-1234

Ungermann Bass, Inc.
5080 Spectrum Dr. #801W
Dallas, TX 75248
214-385-7090

Wang Laboratories, Inc.
One Industrial Way
Lowell, MA 01851

Western Digital Corp.
8105 Irvine Center Dr.
Irvine, CA 92718
214-991-6800

Wollongong Group, Inc.
1129 San Antonio Rd.
Palo Alto, CA 94303
800-872-8649

Wordperfect Corp.
1555 N. Technology Way
Orem, UT 84057
801-225-5000

Zenith Data Systems
1000 Milwaukee Ave.
Glenview, IL
214-323-1010

Wordstar
201 Alameda Del Prado
Novato, CA 94948
800-227-5609

Zoltrix, Inc.
41394 Christy St.
Fremont, CA 94538
510-657-1188

Xerox/Ventura
475 Oakmead Pkwy.
Sunnyvale, CA 94086
408-737-4652

Zylab Corp.
233 E. Erie
Chicago, IL 60611
312-642-2201

XTree Company
14 Inverness Drive East
Inglewood, CO 80112
800-634-5544

PUBLICATIONS AND JOURNALS

Byte
One Phoenix Mill Lane
Peterborough, NH 03458
603-924-9281

Computerworld
375 Cochituate Rd.
Framingham, MA 01701
508-879-0700

CIO
492 Old Connecticut Path
Framingham, MA 01701
508-935-4314

Corporate Computing
950 Tower Lane
Foster City, CA 94404
415-578-7600

Compute!
324 West Wendover Ave.
Greensboro, NC 27408
919-275-9809

Datamation
275 Washington St.
Newton, MA 02158
617-964-3030

Computer Buyer's Guide & Handbook
150 Fifth Ave., #714
New York, NY 10011
212-807-8220

Dr. Dobb's Journal of Software Tools
411 Borel Ave., #100
San Mateo, CA 94402
415-358-9500

Computer Buying World
401 Edgewater Place, #630
Wakefield, MA 01880
617-246-3800

Home Computing Journal
PO Box 21910
Eugene, OR 97402
503-342-4013

Computer Currents
5720 Hollis St.
Emeryville, CA 94608
415-547-6800

Home Office Computing
730 Broadway
New York, NY 10003
212-505-3580

Computerized Investing
625 N. Michigan Ave.
Chicago, IL 60611
312-280-0170

InfoWorld
155 Bovet Rd.
San Mateo, CA 94402
415-572-7341

LAN TIMES
7050 Union Park Center, #240
Midvale, UT 84047
801-565-1060

Lotus Magazine
One Cambridge Center, 5th Floor
Cambridge, MA 02142
617-494-1192

MacUser
950 Tower Lane, 18th Floor
Foster City, CA 94404
415-378-5600

MacWEEK
301 Howard St.
San Francisco, CA 94105
415-243-3500

MacWorld
502 Second St., #600
San Francisco, CA 94107
415-243-0505

MicroPublishing Report
21150 Hawthorne Blvd., #104
Torrance, CA 90503
213-371-5787

MicroTimes
3470 Buskirk Ave.
Pleasant Hill, CA 94523
415-934-3700

Mobile Office
21600 Oxnard St., #480
Woodland Hills, CA 91367
818-593-6100

Network Computing
600 Community Dr.
Manhasset, NY 11030
516-562-5833

NeXTWORLD
501 Second St.
San Francisco, CA 94107
415-978-3191

OS/2 Review
65 Columbia St.
Wood Ridge, NJ 07075

PC/Computing
950 Tower Lane
Foster City, CA 94404
415-578-7000

Pen
PO Box 192566
San Francisco, CA 94119
415-474-6761

Personal Workstation
501 Galveston Rd.
Redwood City, CA 94063
415-366-3600

Shareware Magazine
1030-D East Duane Ave.
Sunnyvale, CA 94086
408-730-9291

Software Digest Ratings Report
625 Ridge Pike
Conshohocken, PA 19428
215-941-9600

Software Magazine
1900 W. Park Dr.
Westborough Office Park
Westborough, MA 01581
508-366-8104

Unix Review
600 Harrison St.
San Francisco, CA 94107
415-397-1881

Unix/World
444 Castro St.
Mountain View, CA 94041
415-940-1500

Window User
25 West 39th St.
New York, NY 10018
212-302-2626

Windows Magazine
PO Box 386
Carpenteria, CA 93014-0385
805-566-1282

SELF-HELP ORGANIZATIONS AND CLUBS

In addition to books, magazines and help from retailers and consultants, there are a great many "self-help" organizations in which ordinary computer users band together to share their knowledge and experience, and to bring newcomers up to speed. You can find information on these "user groups" in local computer publications, and also by asking local retailers and vendors to provide contacts.

SHAREWARE SOURCES

In addition to software made available through traditional commercial channels, you can often find good quality "shareware" with which to automate some of your business processes. Shareware is software that authors and vendors offer on a free trial basis, and for which they typically ask much smaller payment than the software packages with which you are probably more familiar. Shareware is not packaged, not heavily advertised or promoted, and not backed up with the same level of technical support you may get from more prominent software vendors. Yet there are hundreds of shareware packages that are well known, proven in the business world, and as fully capable as any software you can purchase for much higher prices.

Following is a list of some prominent shareware distributors. Call or write to request a catalog, then send for the packages you want to try. The cost is generally only a few dollars per disk. If you like the software package, you send a further payment to the originator or publisher, according to directions given with the shareware itself.

Since shareware is not written to generate huge profits from mass markets, you will likely find these packages were written by experts in particular fields who needed software to do a special-purpose job or modify a particular computer routine. If you have special requirements and do not want custom software, shareware may provide a suitable alternative.

GK Shareware Enterprises
8634 W. National Ave.
West Allis, WI 533227

PC-SIG
1030D East Duane Ave.
Sunnyvale, CA 94086
800-245-6717

Public Brand Software
PO Box 51315
Indianapolis, IN 46251

Reasonable Solutions
2101 West Main St.
Medford, OR 97501

Public Software Library
PO Box 35705
Houston, TX 77235
713-665-7017

Glossary

Access: to make use of, particularly to open a file or to work with an application program or a data file. Example: "She accessed the database and found the information she wanted."

Activate: to execute a computer function, or one of a series of computer commands currently available.

Adapter: the removable hardware that can be added to the internal circuitry of a computer system. Each adapter contains circuits to perform specific functions or support specific external devices.

Append: to add information at the end of an existing data file.

Application: a particular use of a computer, such as for accounting or word processing; also, the software that enables a computer to be used in a particular way or for a particular purpose.

Architecture: the interior physical and logical design of the computer and how its components connect together.

ASCII (American Standard for Computer Information Interchange): a standardized set of codes for representing numbers and characters to which virtually all computers conform; also, a standardized file format incorporating these codes which can be recognized by many different software packages, thus allowing data to be moved electronically from one software package to another.

Automate: computerize, arrange to be done by a computer.

Automatic: to perform a function or task entirely under computer control.

Back up: to store data in more than one place, so that if it is damaged or destroyed, the data can be retrieved from another identical copy; also, the term refers to the second and subsequent copies of files, as in: "Hand me that backup file, will you?"

BASIC: a simplified computer programming language useful for understanding how computers operate internally, and for coding relatively small, simple applications.

Batch: a number of related or similar transactions or operations the computer processes sequentially, usually without the user issuing further commands until the batch process is complete.

Benchmark: a performance standard against which a computer can be measured. "To benchmark" is to test a computer and establish its level of performance.

Bin: a container on a printer that holds blank paper prior to printing.

Bit: the smallest unit of computer information. Eight bits (called a "byte") are required to store a single letter, number or code.

Bitmap: visual information stored in a computer system with every pixel specified, rather than by means of instructions for how to draw the graphics.

Boilerplate: text you reuse in whole or in part, often in combination with new material, to create documents more accurately, easily and rapidly than you otherwise could.

Boot: start operating, the process immediately following power-on by which a computer automatically tests its systems, loads instructions, and begins to perform the various functions for which it is programmed.

Buffer: a portion of computer memory reserved to interrupt the normal flow of information within the computer system. The buffer accepts information from a source, holds it temporarily, then sends it on to its usual destination. This buffering allows the computer system to operate more efficiently and/or gives the user greater control over the information flowing within the computer system.

Bug: a flaw or error in computer software or hardware that interferes with desired operations. The term arose when flies and beetles physically interfered with the operations of the relatively large mechanical components used in the first computer systems.

Bulletin board: a computerized system set up to receive calls from other computers, establish a communications link, and then exchange messages and files between the two computers. Most bulletin board systems can receive calls from more than one computer at a time, and provide a limited menu of commands so the bulletin board—generally operating without a user at the console—can send and receive files under control of the caller.

Bundle: the practice of selling two or more products at one time, as in: "XYZ company now bundles the ABC word processing package with its computer."

Byte: a unit of computer information made up of eight bits, enough to contain a single letter or number. Also, a measurement of computer capacity, as in, "This disk can hold 50 megabytes of information," or, "This computer has 1 megabyte of memory."

Cable: any one of dozens of special sets of wires used to connect together various portions of computer systems.

Cache: a dedicated memory space or a portion of computer memory allocated to temporary, short-term storage of data moving within the computer system. Generally, the cache provides faster storage and retrieval than ordinary memory or long-term storage devices, so the central processor can retrieve information that happens to be in the cache much faster than from anywhere else. Properly sized and controlled cache memory greatly improves computer performance for many tasks, particularly database and computational operations.

CAD (Computer Aided Design): software that helps product designers do their drawings and computations, and that often communicates with other computers to improve the subsequent processes; also, the process of using this software.

CAE (Computer Aided Engineering): software that helps engineers design machines, parts, circuits, and other finished products, and that often communicates with other computers to improve the subsequent processes; also, the process of using this software.

CAM (Computer Aided Manufacturing): integrated software and hardware systems that allow design and/or engineering specifications to directly control the actions of manufacturing equipment; also, the process of using this software.

Cassette: another word for the paper storage bin on a printer; on a tape drive it is the cartridge that holds the data storage tape.

Cell: a location within an electronic spreadsheet defined by the intersection of a column and a row, into which you can enter a label, a number or a formula.

Cell reference: a cell location used in an electronic spreadsheet formula rather than a specific value. When the software calculates the formula, it uses whatever value is presently contained in the referenced cell.

Chip: a small piece of silicon covered with electrical circuits. A chip can contain a central processor, computer memory or specialized circuits that simply replace ordinary electrical wires.

Click: the act of pressing a button on a mouse device.

Clip: a computer function allowing you to highlight a portion of text or of an image, and to copy, move, manipulate, or delete it as though it were separate from the rest of the document or image.

Clip art: simplified standard drawings for use in graphic work. Originally available on paper, clip art is now available as data files for graphics software.

Close: to end computer use of a data file, as in "close a file."

Code: the written computer instructions that make up computer software; also, specialized characters used inside some data files by software.

Command: an instruction given to the computer, usually by a user, and usually in the form of a keystroke or a mouse point-and-click operation.

Command keystroke: a keystroke or sequence of keystrokes that gives the computer a command.

Compatible: a technical term meaning that one element of a computer system can function as intended with another element or with the entire computer system.

Compression: orderly reduction in the amount of computer memory or storage space occupied by a given amount of computerized information.

Configuration: the arrangement and sizes of hardware components, software capabilities, and the resulting computer functions within a single computer or a network of computers. To "configure a computer" is to set up or modify this arrangement.

Connectivity: the quality and/or performance of the connection between two or more computers. Thus, "good connectivity" implies that the computers under discussion can exchange information quickly and easily.

Console: a largely anachronistic term for the desktop work area in which the computer keyboard and display screen are normally used. Example: "Sit at the console and type these letters."

Context-sensitive: describes an on-line help system that automatically provides information relevant to the present state/operation of the software system providing the on-line help. Thus, if you are entering new tab stops into a word processing document, selecting "Help" would bring up information about tab stops.

Corrupt: synonym for damage, as in "a power failure could corrupt this data file and make it useless."

CPU (Central processor unit): the main computer circuitry that executes software instructions and controls the other parts of the system.

Crash: fail or stop working, as in "That new software made my system crash, so I don't use it."

Crunch: calculate or mathematically evaluate, as in "Let the computer crunch these numbers for you."

Cursor: the pointer on the computer's display screen that shows exactly where the computer will next place or remove a character, execute a command, or otherwise direct its attention.

Custom: hardware or software products that are specifically designed, built and/or tailored to the needs of a particular user. Custom hardware is relatively rare. Custom software is less rare, but fraught with danger. It is generally too expensive for small-business applications.

Cut sheet: a plain piece of paper, without tractor feed holes.

Cut over: to switch from one system to another.

Data: raw information, not necessarily in meaningful order.

Data point: any one value in a data set.

Data set: any group of numbers that go together, such as the quarterly profit of a business, or the number of units sold each day during a month or a season.

Database: a collection of information. Databases can include all your customers and their history of purchases, a mailing address or telephone listing, or anything else. In practice, most databases are very well organized and used with computer software that makes it easy to select, sort, and retrieve any item of information.

Database printing: the process of automatically formatting and printing the contents of a database. Most useful for large documents such as telephone directories.

Decompression: orderly expansion of previously compressed computerized information to the full amount of computer memory or storage space it originally occupied.

Daisy wheel: a printing device that can print only letters and numbers of fixed sizes and shapes, contained on a removable wheel, at given positions relative to each other on the page. This contrasts with a "page printer," which can print any shape anywhere on a page.

Decryption: the conversion of coded text to plain text.

Developer: the programmer, vendor or originator of a software package.

Desktop: a size designation for computer equipment, meaning the equipment is roughly small enough to fit on top of a standard office desk.

Dialog box: a small window that appears on a computer screen with blanks you fill in as a means of giving the computer system a command.

Digitize: to convert an image, sound, or other piece of information into digital form, made up of thousands or millions of bits of computer information, and thus capable of being stored, reproduced, or manipulated by a computer.

Disk: the circular storage media on which computers write information for long-term storage. The term "disk" can refer either to the removable "floppy disk" on which the computer can store data, or (more often) to the entire "hard disk" storage device that has much more capacity and speed than the "floppy disk" storage devices on which computers once relied. Disk storage devices can use magnetic or optical technology.

Disk-less work station: a computer without disk drives that relies on the data storage, but not the active memory, of a computer or network to which it is connected.

Display: present information to be seen by the user, usually on a TV-like screen attached to the computer; also, the device on which this information is presented.

Document: a letter, memo, report, presentation or other unified set of information. It can be kept in its own file, or can be kept in a file with other documents.

Dot-matrix printer: a device that uses tiny hammers and an inked ribbon to print closely spaced dots on paper. Early dot-matrix printers were of relatively poor quality. Newer technological advances permit dot-matrix printers to print at or near the "letter quality" standard for characters. Dot-matrix printers fitted with the proper chips are capable of printing graphics.

Down: non-operational, broken.

Download: to receive information on one computer from another computer.

Downtime: the amount of time, or percentage of time, during which a unit or a function is nonoperational.

Downward compatibility: a term describing hardware or software products that can be used with older, but not necessarily newer versions of the same products.

Drive: (noun) the housing, motor, and equipment associated with disk or tape storage devices. Thus a "drive" for a floppy disk would be the unit into which you insert the floppy disk. A "hard drive" would be the entire data storage unit.

Drive: (verb) to serve as the leading or most important element in a situation. Example: "The need for good sales order tracking is what drives our decision to install this computer system."

Duty cycle: the typical or average amount of time a device can operate, or the amount of work it can handle, before it requires normal service or replacement.

Edit: to modify information.

Electronic mail: a simplified system of networking software and hardware that allows notes, memos, letters or larger documents to move from one user's computer to another quickly and easily. Also, the notes or other files sent in this manner. Often abbreviated as "e-mail."

Element: a portion or part of a complete unit. Examples: The display screen is one element of a computer system. The plus sign is one element of a mathematical formula.

Emphatic: a visual, audio, or other element that increases the emphasis and audience impact of material being presented.

Encryption: the conversion of plain text to coded text, usually for security purposes.

End user: a person at the console actually operating a computer.

Engine: a hardware or software device that does a simple job, usually under the control of more sophisticated hardware or software. Thus many different printers may be built around a single type of hardware "print engine," and many different user interfaces may be connected to a single type of software "database engine."

Enter: to load, copy, type, or otherwise provide information to a computer system; also, the key labeled "Return," "Send," or "Enter," on the keyboard, which signals the computer to process the most recent sequence of keystrokes or other computer inputs.

Export: to send information out of a software package, usually in a standardized file format so it can more easily be utilized by other software.

Extract: to copy a portion of the information from an existing data file into a software application.

Feedback: information that is used to control or modify an earlier process in the same sequence. Also, the situation where this occurs. Example: Feedback from the printer tells the computer when to process the next record.

Field: one element of data within a database file. Example: A person's name within a mailing list file.

File: a set of information generally saved and retrieved as a unit by the computer. A file can contain one document or several different documents.

File format: the internal arrangement of the characters and/or software codes in a computer file that make it suitable for use with a particular software program or class of programs.

File server: on a network, a computer dedicated to storing data and program files for use by other computers on the same network.

File sharing: a capability for two or more users to open and manipulate a single data file.

Flat file program: database software that can make entries into, or retrieve from, only one data file at a time. The advantage of this approach is relative ease in learning and using the software.

Flow chart: a diagram that contains various business entities or processes, indicates their relationships to one another, and shows the direction, volume and content of the information (perhaps along with the goods and services) that flows between them.

Footer: the line or lines of text printed at the bottom on every page of a document.

Font: a specific typeface printed or displayed in a specific size.

Format: to prepare a storage disk for use by the computer. Also, the arrangement of data and computer codes in a file. Also, the appearance of a document or portion thereof. Also, to arrange the appearance of a document.

Formatting codes: computer commands inserted into a word processing or other data file that control the appearance of the file when printed. Formatting codes may or may not appear on the display screen.

Formatting pattern: a general set of formatting rules the computer can automatically apply to any (usually extensive) set of data it processes (usually for printing). Also, a style sheet.

Formula: a mathematical sentence used in electronic spreadsheet software to tell the computer what mathematical operations to perform on specified data.

Function: a characteristic, operation or action of a computer. For example, one computer function is to read information from a storage device; another function is to accept input from the keyboard. "To function" is to operate within acceptable performance standards.

Functionality: the characteristics, operations, or actions of a computer system, or the capacity of a computer system to perform desired functions.

Giga: one billion, as in "gigabyte."

Global: pertaining to every instance within a document or a larger computer system. A user can order a global change just once, say from Smith to Smythe, and the computer will make the change dozens or even hundreds of times within one or more documents.

Graphical user interface: a means of controlling a computer with a pointer device and on-screen pictures, or icons, that represent specific computer functions, programs and even data files. GUIs are thought to be far easier to learn and use than "text based interfaces" which require the user to type word commands that follow highly specific rules and syntax.

Graphics: a general term describing a) charts, tables, X-Y graphs, bar graphs, and other visual representations of numeric data, or b) flow charts, organizational charts and other visual representations of relationships between people, events or things, or c) the visual use of typefaces and type sizes, lines, shapes, colors, icons and other elements. All these graphics can now be produced and/or used on the computer display screen, or can be printed by the computer on paper. Example: "This mapping program has great graphics!" "This graphics program makes great charts."

Graphics printer: a computer printer capable of printing computer graphics.

Hacker: a person who exhibits a great deal of computer expertise, often achieved by spending a great deal of time using computers, and who enjoys exploring new computer software, hardware and systems, even if uninvited to do so. "Hackers gained access to our system last night and searched our data."

Hard copy: printed material.

Hardware: the physical elements that make up the computer system, such as the processor, the keyboard, the monitor, the disk drives, the memory and the printer.

Header: the line or lines of text printed at the top on every page of a document.

Help: directions on computer system capabilities, procedures, terminology, commands and/or next steps for users to take, designed to help a user operate a software and/or hardware system.

Hertz: unit of measurement equal to one cycle per second.

High-end: refers to the most powerful, sophisticated, or expensive items within a range of roughly similar or comparable computer products.

Highlight: to temporarily change the color or gray tone of a portion of the information displayed on a computer screen as a means of indicating exactly which material the computer will selectively manipulate or activate.

Host: in a system of two or more devices, the host is the computer supporting or controlling the other device(s).

Human interface: the means by which a computer system exchanges information with users.

Ibid: the time-saving and error-saving capability of a computer system, usually database software, to copy previous input to a new location when the user presses a simple keystroke combination.

Icons: small, stylized pictures of things, actions and words that are used to represent specific computer functions, programs and data files in a graphical user interface.

Image: information contained in pixels.

Import: to read information into a software package from an electronic data file; usually one in a relatively standardized format.

Information: usually refers to data in a meaningful organization, but can be broadly defined or used abstractly to refer to messages, items, ideas, structures, locations, and so forth.

Input: information fed into a system, or the act of feeding information into a computer system.

Input station: a computer terminal or console set up so data can easily be entered into a computer system.

Insert: to add new information in the midst of old information—on disk or in computer memory.

Install: to copy software onto the storage device of a computer so it can be activated to provide its intended functions. Also, to make internal adjustments to software and/or hardware so it operates as intended with other elements in the computer system.

Integrate: to make all required changes or adjustments so that separate computer elements or systems can function together as a single, larger system.

Interchange: to exchange or transfer (usually data) from one software package to another. Example: "This software can easily interchange data with that software."

Interface: the means by which two systems, or one system and a user, exchange information.

Key: a button on a keyboard, the act of pressing such a button.

Key word: a sequence of characters within a word, sentence, paragraph or document that (at the user's command) the software marks for special attention, so that subsequently it can search for and locate a particular key word much more quickly than another word not specially marked.

Keyboard: the set of typewriter-like keys used for data input and for issuing commands to the computer, usually mounted on a single panel or board. Also, "to keyboard" is to enter data or commands by means of the keyboard.

Keypress: keystroke.

Keystroke: the press of a single key on the computer's keyboard.

Kilo: unit of measurement equal to one thousand.

Label: any text entered into an electronic spreadsheet cell not for use in spreadsheet computations. Also, text superimposed on a business graph to indicate the meaning of a particular axis, data point or data set.

Laptop: a size designation for computer equipment, meaning the equipment is small and light enough to be balanced on the user's knees or lap while sitting and working.

Laser printer: a computer printer that uses a laser beam to etch an image of great clarity, resolution and flexibility. Laser printers can print both "letter quality" characters and "graphics" quality images.

Letter quality: a designation for computer printers capable of producing characters at least as clear, clean and well formed as those from a standard office typewriter.

Link: to establish a communications pathway between two computers (or two software packages on a single computer) so that data flows automatically across the link, or so that the user can instantly change the display and the computer's capabilities to reflect what is at either end of the link.

Load: copy computer data from one location to another, as in: "Load the software from the floppy disk onto the hard disk," or, "Load the data into computer memory."

Logical: pertains to the computer's organization of information. That is, the computer may divide one physical disk drive into two or more logical drives that it will treat as entirely separate devices.

Look up table: a prepared data table the computer uses to compare one value to another, so that when given—for example—a part number, the computer also knows the price, the shipping weight and/or other information about the specific part. To "look up" is to refer to such a "look-up table."

Loop: a sequence of computer instructions that causes the computer to repeat the sequence at least once, but possibly without end.

Low end: refers to the least powerful, sophisticated or expensive items within a range of roughly similar or comparable computer products.

Macro: a relatively complex set of computer commands stored inside the computer, and called up for execution with a relatively short command. Macro capabilities can cover keyboard, mouse and other inputs, and can be built into application software or can be supplied by specially designed utility software.

Mail merge: the automated capability to create individualized letters or other documents by reprinting an original data file many times, each time placing into specified locations within the main text a new set of variable information copied from a separate data file. This capability is most frequently delivered as part of a word processing software package. The most common usage would be to print hundreds of letters, each basically identical but individually addressed to specific people.

Manually: to perform a function or task—whether digging a ditch or issuing commands that control the performance of a computer—in person and in real time (that is, by hand).

Mega: unit of measurement equal to one million.

Memory: the random access memory of a computer used to contain both data and software instructions. For most computer systems, the memory is erased when the power is turned off.

Menu: a list (usually on-screen) of commands to which computer software will respond. The user simply selects one option from the menu, and the computer executes the associated commands or shifts to a submenu with additional options. Menus are widely regarded as a relatively simple means of controlling an otherwise difficult program.

Menu driven: describes a software package operated by means of menus.

Migration path: the term for newer, better, more powerful software or hardware to which you can easily move your data, your computer applications and your knowledge of computer procedures when existing software or hardware no longer meets your needs.

Mode: type of operation, as in: "The word processing software starts out in insert mode, but you can switch it to overwrite mode with a simple keystroke."

Model: a set of mathematical formulas and values that—when correctly designed and implemented—compute approximately the same results from a given input value or set of values as would be produced by the real-life system the model is intended to emulate. For example, a model intended to emulate an office building would compute the bottom-line results expected from the actual building when operated with specified rents, occupancy rates, and annual operating expenses.

Modem: a device that allows a computer to exchange signals over standard telephone lines with another computer also equipped with a compatible modem, short for "modulator/demodulator."

Module: a unified piece of hardware or software that performs a specific function or series of functions, as in: "The second software module handles everything the first module doesn't," or, "The hard drive is housed in a small, self-contained module."

Mouse: a palm-sized device that a user can move across the surface of a table or desk. Moving the mouse causes the on-screen cursor to move a corresponding distance and direction. Pressing the mouse button(s) issues a command to the computer that is partly based on the on-screen position of the cursor. Mouse-type controllers are often used, and sometimes required, for graphical user interfaces and/or graphics software.

Multi-tasking: the ability of a computer system to support two or more applications operating at the same time.

Nanosecond: one billionth of a second.

Network: a communications system that allows two or more computers to exchange data and program files, and may also allow one computer to run software that resides on another.

Object: a computer term describing a unified graphic or program element that can be copied, modified or deleted without disturbing other "objects" within the graphic image or program code.

OCR (optical character recognition): the computer's process of recognizing patterns in an image as letters and/or numbers. OCR software can convert image files to text files, and vice versa.

Off-line: describes the situation when data or computer capabilities are not immediately available to the computer system. To make them available, physical connections must be made; tapes, disks or other data storage media must be physically loaded into drives, or communication links must be established.

Off-the-shelf: describes hardware and software products that can be purchased in standard configurations for immediate installation and use.

On-line: describes the situation when data or computer capabilities are presently connected and thus immediately available within the computer system.

On the network: refers to computer hardware and software correctly connected to a computer network system, and thus accessible to users of other computers similarly connected.

Open: to initiate computer use of a data file, as in: "Open a file." Also, non-proprietary and thus available for use in many different vendors' computer products.

Open system: describes any form of computer technology that is not owned, patented or protected by any one vendor or manufacturer, and thus is generally available from several different vendors. Antonym: "proprietary."

Operating system: a critical piece of computer software that controls how the central processor will utilize the various hardware components connected to it, and that also sets requirements for running application software on the system. A particular central processor can usually support several different operating systems (although usually only one at a time).

Operation: a computer function or process that results in a change of condition within a computer system.

Outliner: a software package (generally a word processor) providing outline manipulation capabilities.

Overlay: new information or computer commands replacing or adding to previous ones. Example: "Let's overlay this information on that." Or: "Use this overlay next." Also, to superimpose some graphic images on others.

Output: information delivered or produced by a computer system, or the act of delivering or producing information.

Overwrite: to replace old information—on disk or in computer memory—with new information.

Package: a unified collection of software that works in harmony to provide particular computer functions or capabilities, such as word processing, accounting, or desktop publishing. "Package" may also refer to a single piece of application software, or to an integrated system of hardware components, with or without associated software.

Page description language: a set of codes by which a computer and printer communicate the information to be printed.

Page printer: a device capable of printing any shape anywhere on a page. Page printers normally use laser, ink-jet, dot-matrix, or similar technology. This contrasts with "daisy-wheel" or other typewriter-like technology that can print only letters and numbers of fixed sizes and shapes at given positions relative to each other.

Paper-based: printed on paper rather than stored in computerized form. Example: "My paper-based records take up 15 file cabinets, but if I converted them to computer they'd fit into the top drawer of my desk."

Pixel: "picture element," the tiniest piece of a computerized image that can be displayed or printed; ordinarily a single dot on the display screen or a printed picture. Computer images can contain up to one million or more pixels.

Point-and-click: mouse device operation in which the user moves the mouse to place the computer's cursor where desired and then presses a button on the mouse.

Pop up: usually refers to a menu, dialog box, or software that appears on the screen during a software operation, allowing you to make a choice or issue a command before it disappears and returns the screen to its previous appearance.

Port: a location within a computer system's circuitry where an output device may be connected.

Portable: a size designation for computer equipment, meaning the equipment is smaller than "desktop size," but larger than "laptop size."

Portfolio: selection or repertoire, as in: "You have a good portfolio of application software."

Power: a rough measure of the computer's capacity to store and manipulate data, or to perform sophisticated computer operations. Example: "This new computer has more power to calculate our large spreadsheet models than the old one."

Power off: turn off or remove electrical power from.

Power on: turn on or provide electrical power for.

Preprogram: to program a computer operation or keystroke sequence— normally by a user—to simplify making use of it later on.

Price-performance curve: a highly generalized business graphic, rarely drawn but often discussed, which quantifies how the speed, power and other capabilities of computers increase for systems with higher prices. There is a range high on the price-performance curve where higher prices do not bring commensurate performance increases. There is also a range low on the price-performance curve where a few extra dollars purchase a significant amount of additional performance.

Printer control language: a less sophisticated page description language that serves essentially the same purpose, but may take longer and offer fewer options or less control over details.

Print time: the time when a document is printed. Also, the amount of time required to print a given document.

Procedure: a linked and coordinated series of actions or tasks taken to achieve a specific purpose or accomplish a specific goal. In computers, "procedures" usually involve an ordered series of keystroke or mouse commands that cause the computer to perform a specific job.

Process: a computer function or operation that results in a change of condition within the computer system.

Production system: a computer system that uses real business data and supports day-to-day business operations. Antonym: "prototype" system.

Program: a set of software instructions that together perform a specific task or allow a computer to be used for a specific application. Also, the act of giving a computer instructions. Examples: "This program is very powerful." "Please program the computer to add 2 and 2."

Prompt: an inquiry symbol or word question the computer displays to the user, in effect asking for input. Also, "to prompt" is to display such a symbol or question.

Proprietary: describes any form of computer technology that is owned, patented or protected by a particular vendor or manufacturer, and thus available only from that one source. Antonym: "open system."

Prototype system: software meant only to demonstrate how a production system will operate. The prototype system lacks the power, the capacity or the actual computer code to support day-to-day business operations. Antonym: "production" system.

Pull down: usually refers to menus that drop from the top of the screen when selected by keystroke or mouse click, allowing you to choose among menu options for controlling the computer's subsequent operation. Once a choice is made, the pull down menu disappears and returns the screen to its previous appearance.

Pull up: retrieve.

Punch: to enter data, usually into a computer using a conventional computer keyboard. Example: "Sit at the keyboard and punch these names and addresses into the database, please." This term arose because cards punched with many holes at highly specific locations were one of the first means of storing and loading computer information.

Punch-up: pull up.

RAM (Random Access Memory): the computer's main memory space for programs and data.

Read: import, load or copy data from long-term storage into computer memory.

Record: a unit of information within a database manager. Example: each record contains a complete name and address within a long list of many names and addresses. Also, to store information for later retrieval.

Real time: at the same time as a normal, related occurrence takes place. Example: You drive a car in real time (as it moves along the street), and you make an oral presentation in real time (as the accompanying slides flash on the screen and as people listen to your words), but you don't write a report in real time because you normally write a draft and make changes at your convenience later on.

Relational program: database software that can make entries into, or retrieve from, more than one data file at a time. The advantage of this approach is greater efficiency in storing data and more flexibility in working with the information.

Remote control: the process of linking two computers so they operate as if they were one. Both computers will run software installed on either one, data typed on either keyboard enters both computers simultaneously, and identical displays are generated simultaneously on both screens. Data can be output on a printer, network or other device connected to either computer.

Report: a printed or displayed or electronically stored listing of, about, or derived from some or all of the information controlled by the application software; most often database software. For example, a report generated by a database program may list 50 records from the data file that meet certain specifications, or the report may describe the number of records and the field sizes contained in the data file, or the report may calculate for each record the mathematical sum or the product of numbers contained in specified fields of the data file.

Report specification: the proper commands in the proper order that cause a database application to generate a desired report. Some software allows a report specification to be saved on disk and used many times to generate reports over and over again, each with the latest available data.

Reserved: removed from general usage and dedicated to a special purpose or task. Most often used to describe keystrokes or keystroke combinations associated with particular software functions. For example, the arrow keys are almost always reserved for cursor movement, while the "alternate-equal sign" keystroke combination is often reserved for keyboard macro software.

Reside: describes the situation when software is stored in a particular location, as in: "The software resides on computer A, but can be used over the network from computer B."

Retrieve: fetch, get or otherwise find specific computerized data and display or utilize it in subsequent operations.

ROM (Read Only Memory): the computer's permanent memory space—not erased at power-off—for start-up routines and other internal process instructions.

Routine: a set of computer instructions and/or procedures organized to accomplish a particular task or purpose. Example: "The software contains routines for data analysis."

Run: operate or start, as in "The software runs only on IBM-type computers," or, "Run the software, then load the data."

Run time: the time when a software package is started on a computer. Also, the length of time a batch process requires to finish; also describes a piece of software used to provide some, but not all, of the capabilities of a complete software package. Examples: "Run time is tomorrow at noon." "The run time for this batch is about three hours." "This run time module allows us to display on our clients' computers the slide shows we create here in the home office with our presentation package."

Scalable: refers to technology that operates in virtually any scale or size. Most common usage is "scalable fonts," which can be printed in any size. Can also refer to scalable software systems, which will operate on micro, mini or mainframe computers with equal ease.

Scan: to enter information into a computer system by means of a device, similar to a copier, which converts any visual image to computerized bitmapped form, including material typed, printed, or handwritten on a piece of paper or another flat surface.

Scanner: a computer input device, similar to the top half of a copy machine or a hand-held bar-code reader, which scans.

Screen: the name for a set of information, text and/or graphics that appears at one time on the computer display screen, as in: "That screen contains everything we need to know." Also, the processing of sifting through a large amount of information and retaining only that which is relevant, as in: "Screen this database for people who are named George." Also, the computer's display screen.

Search: to compare, or to have the computer compare, some or all of the data in a file or in memory against a specific (often incomplete) search phrase.

Search phrase: a sequence of characters and/or numbers you enter at the beginning of a computer search. Example: "Find the search phrase 'Alger' within a list of countries." The computer would find Algeria if that name were listed.

Service: a computer operation that simplifies or supports a specific task, such as file storage and retrieval, communications or number crunching.

Simulation: an elaborate computer model that provides highly detailed results approximating the results to be expected from the real-life system being simulated. Computer simulations often utilize sophisticated display and physical motion hardware to provide realistic visual images and sensations of movement—as in computerized flight simulators or amusement park "ride" simulators.

Software: the instructions that make the hardware perform specific tasks or respond to specific commands. Operating system software specifies and controls the basic functions of the computer. Environment or interface software dictates how the computer presents you with information and takes your commands. Application software makes the computer perform a specific task, such as word processing, project management or accounting.

Software package: describes one or more pieces of software that are delivered together, and which generally provide a unified system of computer functions.

Sort: to have the computer change the order of data in a file or in memory. Example: "Sort a list of names and addresses alphabetically, according to last name."

Speed: a rough measure of how quickly the computer processes data or commands, often measured in megahertz.

Storage system: a hardware device within a computer system in which files can be stored for long periods of time, even when the power is turned off.

Style sheet: formatting codes or commands stored in a computer file that are separate from a document's contents, allowing one style sheet to be swapped for another at any time, making it very easy to change the printed or on-screen appearance of a complex document without reformatting it page by page.

Subsystem: an alternate term for a computer device, such as data storage or display, which is completely contained within a larger computer system.

Support: either human or technical structures or services that tend to facilitate or allow for, as in: "Computers support rapid information retrieval." "That company provides a technical support telephone hot line for its software." "This accounting package supports as many as 15 different checking accounts."

System: a generic term that applies to one or more components of computer hardware and/or software that completely fulfills a particular need. Thus a computer system can be a complete outfit of compatible hardware and software, or it can be a network of dozens of independent computers that work together to provide a very complex employee support capability. An accounting system can be a software package that provides a full range of accounting functions or a series of communicating computers that separately handle accounting for different parts of a business. A communications system can be a modem and appropriate software to permit computerized communications or a computer controlling communications into and out of an area.

Tape: magnetic recording tape used for computer data storage. The use of magnetic tape requires specialized tape drives, just as the use of disks requires disk drives. (In the first years of computers, strips of paper tape punched with holes in specific locations were used to store information.)

Task: a relatively small, simple or single-purpose computer operation that, in combination with other tasks, adds up to useful work.

Template: a file or style sheet used as a pattern to make sure several different computerized files are duplicates of the original, or at least similar in appearance. Thus a template for a telephone answering message would be a file containing the basic form to be filled in and saved separately from the template, while a template for a presentation would be a file dictating the basic appearance of the finished pages or slides in any number of unique presentations.

Terminal: a computer-like device without data storage and usually without memory that relies on the data storage and memory of a computer or network to which it is connected.

Text: information contained in letters and numbers.

Text based interface: the first generally accepted method of controlling computers. It requires the user to type word commands that follow highly specific rules and syntax.

Threshold: a level of computer capability that meets your processing requirements. Computers below the threshold are unsatisfactorily slow or limited, while those too far over the threshold cost too much to justify the slightly better support they give your applications in comparison to other computers at or just over your threshold requirements.

Throughput: the amount of actual work accomplished by the computer system and its users, taking all human and technological factors into account.

Tool: in computers, a device—often software—designed to make a particular task easier. Examples: An on-screen calculator, a mortgage amortization table printer, a file management program.

Track: to keep track of; keep detailed records on.

Tractor feed: a method for moving a continuous series of pages through a computer printer by means of mechanically moving pins on the printer that fit into and pull on evenly spaced holes in the paper. The continuous stream of pages, and the tractor feed holes, may be easily detached and separated after printing by tearing along perforated lines.

Track ball: a cursor-moving device that consists of a ball free to rotate within a stationary mounting. Rotation of the ball causes the on-screen cursor to move a corresponding distance and direction.

Transfer: to send or receive a file (usually containing only data, not programs) between two software packages or two computers. Example: "This computer can easily transfer files to that one."

Translate: to modify computer coded data or program files from the format required by one software or hardware system to the format required by another.

Tutorial: self-controlled software designed to provide an educational or training experience for the computer user with the aim of helping him or her learn specific knowledge. Tutorials are often used to train a person how to run a software package.

Up: operational.

Update: renew, refresh, or otherwise replace with a later version. For example, old software can be updated with a newer package from the same vendor. Similarly, old information can be updated to reflect recent changes.

Upgrade: replace an existing component of a computer system with a newer version of a software package, or with different, more powerful software or hardware.

Upload: to send information from one computer to another.

Upward compatibility: describes hardware or software products that can be used with newer, but not necessarily older versions of the same products.

User: a person who operates a computer; a computer user; an end user.

User friendly: easy for a person to learn and to operate.

Utility software: the general term for relatively small, single-purpose software often capable of running at the same time as application software. Utility software can repair or prevent disk drive problems, change keyboard and display screen characteristics, make it easier to access and manipulate files on the disk, and do other important tasks within the computer system.

Value: a specific letter, number or other bit of information. Example: "Please read me the value in the first cell of that spreadsheet."

Vector graphics: visual information stored in a computer system by means of instructions for how to draw it, rather than with every pixel specified.

Vendor: the seller of a software or hardware product.

Work station: a location where work is done, or where computerized work is done. Also, the term is often used to refer to a very high-powered computer capable of very high-resolution displays and CAD, CAE, or CAM applications.

Write: (for a computer) transfer information from active memory to storage.

WYSIWYG: acronym for "what you see is what you get," (pronounced "wizzy-wig") refers to the ability of a computer system to display on its screen exactly what it will print on paper.

Resources for Small Businesses

How to Organize Your Work and Your Life, 1993, Robert A. Moskowitz, Bantam Doubleday Dell, 1540 Broadway, New York, NY 10036, (800) 223-6834. In New York State: (212) 354-6500. (Softcover, $14.95)

Upstart Publishing Company, Inc. These publications on proven management techniques for small businesses are available from Upstart Publishing Company, Inc., 12 Portland St., Dover, NH 03820. For a free current catalog, call (800) 235-8866 outside New Hampshire, or 749-5071 in state.

The Business Planning Guide, Sixth edition, 1992, David H. Bangs, Jr. and Upstart Publishing Company, Inc. (Softcover, 208 pp., $19.95) Speadsheet templates using Lotus 1-2-3® or Microsoft Excel® are available for $12.95.

The Market Planning Guide, 1990, David H. Bangs, Jr. and Upstart Publishing Company, Inc. (Softcover, 160 pp., $19.95)

The Cash Flow Control Guide, 1990, David H. Bangs, Jr. and Upstart Publishing Company, Inc. (Softcover, 88 pp., $14.95)

The Personnel Planning Guide, 1988, David H. Bangs, Jr. and Upstart Publishing Company, Inc. (Softcover, 176 pp., $19.95)

The Start Up Guide: A One-Year Plan for Entrepreneurs, 1989, David H. Bangs, Jr. and Upstart Publishing Company, Inc. (Softcover, 160 pp., $19.95)

Managing by the Numbers: Financial Essentials for the Growing Business, 1992, David H. Bangs, Jr. and Upstart Publishing Company, Inc. (Softcover, 160 pp., $19.95)

Borrowing for Your Business, 1991, George M. Dawson (Hardcover, 160 pp., $19.95)

Buy the Right Business—At the Right Price, 1990, Brian Knight and the Associates of Country Business, Inc. (Softcover, 152 pp., $18.95)

The Home-Based Entrepreneur, Second edition, 1993, Linda Pinson and Jerry Jinnett (Softcover, 192 pp. $19.95)

Keeping the Books, 1993, Second edition, Linda Pinson and Jerry Jinnett. (Softcover, 208 pp., $19.95)

Steps to Small Business Start Up, 1993, Linda Pinson and Jerry Jinnett (Softcover, 200 pp., $19.95)

Target Marketing for the Small Business., 1993, Linda Pinson and Jerry Jinnett (Softcover, 208 pp., $19.95)

The Woman Entrepreneur, 1992, Linda Pinson and Jerry Jinnett (Softcover, 244 pp., $14.00)

On Your Own: A Woman's Guide to Starting Your Own Business, Second edition, 1993, Laurie Zuckerman (Softcover, 224 pp., $19.95)

Problem Employees, 1991, Dr. Peter Wylie and Dr. Mardy Grothe (Softcover, 272 pp., $22.95)

Index

Accounting system software, 7-9, 17, 60-64; accounts payable (AP) module, 65; accounts receivable (AR) module, 65-66; chart of accounts, 64; computation and information entry, 39-40; general ledger (GL), 64-65; inventory/purchase order (IPO) module, 68; other modules, 68-69; payroll module (PM), 66-67; point of sale (POS)/invoice writing (IW) module, 6768; sales analysis (SA) module, 66; spreadsheet accounting, 81

Appointment books/schedulers software programs, 126

Artificial intelligence software, 6, 17, 40

Audio capabilities, 121

Backup/protection system, data, 109, 131-132, 153

Boilerplate text/documents, 9, 86, 154

Bulletin board, computerized, 51, 154-155

Business graphics software, 6, 44, 93-95

Cache utilities, 128, 155

Central processor, 108, 157

Charting software, electronic, 6, 45, 96-97

Clubs and self-help organizations, 150

Color printers, 111

Communications, 6, 28; and information sharing, 42-43; need for various types of, 51

Compact disks (CDs), 11

Computer Aided Design (CAD) software, 45, 131, 155

Computer Aided Engineering (CAE) software, 45, 155

Computer Aided Manufacturing (CMA) software, 45, 155

Computer modeling: and simulation, 43-44; spreadsheet application in, 78-79

Computers: computer functions, 26-28; evaluating computer systems, 53-55; factors in choosing a computer system, 22-23; growing with computers in business, 23-25; identifying business computer needs, 29-48; integrating old and new systems, 25; investigating available computer products, 48-53; liabilities of using, 19-22; overview of complete computer system, 25-26; strategic advantages of, 18-19; transition from manual to automated systems, 55; use of computers in business, 1-7; ways to

value